Bail Bonds Babylon

LAURA LANFIELD

This Edition published 2010 by Laura Lanfield
Matanda Publications.
Copyright 2006
Second Revision Published 2006
Third Revision Published 2010

Cover Graphic Provided By: Colin O'Donnell

Printed and bound in the U.S.A.

Although this book is an accurate accounting of some of my bail bonding experiences, I have taken certain artistic liberties and forays into the realm of fiction. For my safety and that of my family and to avoid the risk that could be attached to such a full disclosure, names have been changed and small portions of this book have been fictionalized. For that reason, I must present this very definite disclaimer that any similarity to any events, happenings, situations or persons living or dead, guilty or innocent, is purely and simply coincidental.

Acknowledgements

On this page I have to thank those of you who have chosen for one reason or another to play a part in my evolving into the person who was able to write this story. I'm sure I've missed some, but if I have, remember that I thank you too. First of all, my husband, who has been staunch in his praise and patience throughout this long endeavor. My mother, whom you will read about and come to love as I did. My very supportive, beautiful daughter, who, along with her generous husband, plies me with gifts, wonderful forays into the world of expensive eating places, and escapes to exotic Caribbean islands when this homebound life gets to be too much. My Libra son, capable and worldly, whose affection for me has always been evident. Nick, my lost friend, who encouraged my career and died before my book was born, will never be forgotten. To my grandfather, who knew how bright I was, and who always encouraged me but sadly didn't live to see all of my accomplishments. To my friend Art, who sees things in a spiritual way and encouraged me throughout my most difficult times. To my dear friend and healer, for countless hours of healing my body, mind, and spirit, and allowing me to have the strength and fortitude to write this book. To my wonderful British friend, Fletch, who saw my potential and encouraged me to carry on no matter what. He sharpened me up constantly with daily e-mails that required cogent responses. To my three adorable, generous, amusing, kind and charming brothers for all their love and support. And of course, many thanks to Jeff, my editor who patiently worked with this saucy old broad, corrected and changed and gave me the confidence to see a potential winner come out of this. To my talented capable Personal Assistant Jennifer Vensel for her invaluable help and extreme patience.

Prologue

"You miserable bitch!" He said to me, "It's all your fault!"

His name was Henry. Built like a line-backer, he towered over my petite frame like a bullying, intimidating, dark cloud.

The courtroom was packed. Everyone was sweaty. The tension in the air was at a fever pitch. Judge Goodman glowered from high atop the crowd as he admonished the defendant not to raise his cane and hit the bondsman, me. I was a petite buxom blonde in my early 30s. So naturally, when colossal-sized Henry loomed over me, he looked like he was about to smash an ant. The judge's eyes were blood red with anger. Not in his court would such a thing happen.

The two horrified bailiffs stood close to me as if I were in some sort of protective custody. I guess in a way I was.

Henry, the bastard, was pissed cause he knew his ass was going to jail and he also knew he had me to thank for it.

Not to say he had not warned me before of his violent nature, but I was not going to let this scum bully me like he did others. What the hell was I supposed to do, stand there quietly while this ignorant, rapist smashed my skull as he shouted obscenities about my sex, my race and my occupation? I don't think so.

It was his stream of loudly spoken well-delivered phrases that brought the scene to the judge's attention.

I was paralyzed with fear but I wasn't about to let him know it, not for a second. My piercing blue eyes locked on his cold, very dark, menacing eyes. I stepped up in my bright colored platform shoes, or fuck me pumps as we called them in the '70s, and said through gritted teeth, loud enough only for him to hear, "*YOU* raped them not me. You're going down you miserable bastard."

I knew that was not exactly the language of a lady raised as well as I but when you run across a piece of shit like him, who raped 2 little girls you can tend to get a little hot under the collar. And as the saying goes, "You can wrap a pig in silk but it's still a pig."

Or in my case, "you can wrap a lady in rags but she's still a lady."

As a bondsman the court had released my client, Patricia, into my care, custody and control so I was essentially responsible for her. I escorted her and her two young daughters who were trembling with fear into the courtroom with me. My heart breaks just thinking about how he defiled those girls, their hair braided in barrettes, their sad big eyes getting ever so large at the sight of this horrible man who had stolen their innocence and called himself their father. I knew at that moment there was no way in hell I was going to let him get away with it.

I felt confident that now here in the courtroom, Patricia's safety and that of her two daughters was assured. Never dreamed *my* brains might be bashed in by this lunatic husband of hers. No good deed goes unpunished they say. The shit I had to put up with as a lady bondsman.

Sure, I was a front-runner in the industry, a job born of desperation.

As I stood in the courtroom in that moment, I flashed back to a few desperate months earlier and what led up to my being a bondsman in that courtroom.

I refused to even consider asking my abusive soon-to-be ex-husband for financial support because I hated with a vengeance, the thought of making myself vulnerable to him once again especially when I reminded myself of how he had hurt and humiliated me and my two small children. I had remained in the marriage far too long. I knew that, but, I also knew that I stayed because I felt there was no alternative. I did love Frank, had borne his two children and my sense of commitment to my marriage vows was very strong. There had never been a divorce in my family for as far back as anyone could remember. Coming from a Russian and Norwegian/Finnish background, the sanctity of marriage was very important to us. So I tried to be a good person, took care of my kids and did all the right things. But, when the emotional and physical abuse became so painful even I had to stop and take a long look at what was happening.

One night, when he was drinking heavily, his tongue loosened by the booze, he came over to me in the kitchen as I was preparing dinner and said, "Lori, you really are a piece of shit, you know. What can I do or say that would be bad enough that you would let me go? You're young, and a good fuck and all, but you have no fire, no fight, you once did, but now you bore me to death." I forced a smile and said nothing as he carried yet another drink into the living room and turned on the television. I wanted to tell him right there and then what I was thinking, but I knew it would just give him a good reason to hit me again and I was not emotionally prepared to stand up to him at that time.

I had met Frank when I was only 17 and he was 27. I was attracted by his good looks, his gently persuasive sexuality and sense of humor. For a few years we were divinely happy. But then he started to drink a lot, and all my dreams were shattered and our happy times were over. My marriage had been a disastrous duet for several years. Like a dancing suicide pact, we had two–stepped and shuffled our way through a devastating relationship bonded by our anger and frustration that things had not worked out for us. We blamed each other that our blueprint for happiness had been corrupted by ourselves, the architects of our souls.

It finally came to pass one evening when Frank came home early from work, ushered his handsome self into our kitchen and poured his favorite libation. That, of course was, a shot of Laird's Applejack brandy and a pint of Ballantine ale. A boiler-maker they used to call it. . The house was quiet, the cool crisp November air swept through the open French doors cooling down everything except my passionate disdain of this selfish drunk who was making my life a misery. My 11-year-old daughter, Allison, was at cheerleading practice and nine-year-old son, Chris, was expected home at any moment from his after-school football practice.

I walked into the kitchen and said to Frank, "Do you think you might go into our bedroom for a few minutes? I'd like to talk to you, and the kids will-"

He cut me off with, "Yeah, yeah, yeah. I know, Miss Priss and little Chris can't see their daddy like this," he said in a voice that mocked me.

In spite of his drunkenness I saw a little bit of the old Frank, the Frank I fell in love with. He would have been embarrassed by this terrible behavior.

Frank said nothing else as he teetered across the dining room and suddenly tripped over the step down into the living room. As he fell, the can of ale dropped from his hand to the floor spilling all over, but he managed to hold aloft the small glass of Brandy and as he smirked a drunken smile said to me, "See, I'm pretty steady on me feet, ain't I bitch."

At that exact moment Chris came through the front door with his little football friend Alex and froze at the sight of his dad, who by now had fallen through onto the living room floor, and urinated in his pants. I knew at that moment, what I *had to do*. And soon.

My dream television job was over and I was out on my ass. Reality crowded in on me again. What a cruel joke it seemed, going from fame and glory in the television world to being in a courthouse getting assaulted by an insane defendant whom my brother had bonded out just weeks before.

It was only too real – opening the refrigerator to find only a jar of crusted applesauce that was a month old and what was left of a stale box of raisins. I thought to myself half-joking, "Well, at least I paid the mortgage this month."

And I did it with every penny I could scrounge together because I was too proud to let my mother and rest of my family know how bad things really were.

Ever since Frank left me it had been a struggle to make it financially, my savings were used up, no good job in sight, and although I was determined to win the battle, it looked like I was losing.

I could hear the music of the ice cream truck coming around the corner as I stared at the empty refrigerator. I knew what was next.

"Mom! Mom!" Allison and Chris cried, "Do you got any money?"

"Have any money," I corrected and fished in my pockets, although I knew they were bare. There was only one place I had any cash left, my piggy bank and I had sworn to only use it when absolutely necessary. But I couldn't bear to say, "no" to my kids, not with the other children screaming with excitement at the ice cream truck parked right in front of our house.

I opened the piggy bank and my kids' eyes lit up waiting with anticipation for all the glorious cash. I could barely look into their beautiful blue eyes and was ashamed as only two coins came out, 35 cents.

"But Mom, it's 50 cents." Chris said.

I fought the tears, "I'm sure I have some more money somewhere." I said, searching the drawers for something, anything.

Allison looked at me with sympathy. She cleared her throat, "That's okay Mom. Chris can have it."

I nodded, waiting until they left before my tears burst out like the Goddamn Hoover Dam. I had never felt so low in my life.

No job, no food to feed my children, I was desperate and knew I had to do something.

Chapter One

*T*he Canadians had sent us down a blast of icy air, so it was an unusually cold Miami evening. Christmas was around the corner yet I was as hot and flushed as if I had a high temperature.

I sat in my piece of shit car that should have been junked half a decade ago. I just sat there outside the bar for what seemed like hours knowing that I was about to do something I had sworn never to do. I was at the point of no return and desperation had crept on tiny cat's paws into my every waking thought.

My family had no idea. And I managed a good front. From time to time the kids told my mother this or that about how bad things were at home but I covered very nicely and I had learned that no one really wants to hear your troubles, not even family.

I've always been an independent person. The last thing I wanted was to go to my family for help. After all, my mother had told me more than once, "You made your bed, now lie in it."

It was a point of contention between my mother and I. She did not want me to get a divorce and was very emphatic about it.

"If I could put up with your father, and not divorce him for all those years," she said, "then certainly you can try and make a go of it with Frank."

So, naturally, any help she would give me would be with certain conditions. Trial separation, bullshit, we had tried that. My not working and staying home with the kids, because she thought that Frank was jealous of my being at work. Not a good idea, tried it, did not have enough money without two salaries. It seemed that she also had no solutions.

With no one else to turn to, and rather than go along with all of her ideas and ask my mom for help I decided to bury my pride, risk humiliation and go see my children's father to ask for some money. It was worth a try. Although he was working, had a good job, he had given me no financial support since he left three months before.

My fingers touched the reddened ridge above my left eye brow, a grim reminder of my last encounter with my children's father and prepared myself to do what I knew I had to do.

The Deuce Bar was well known to me; a place where too many nights I had come down as if brought by a magnet to this watering hole in the midst of Miami Beach. This joint that was so attractive to the man I married. So many times I remembered coming there with him to bring him back home with me and the children. But this time was different. I was humiliated by my lack of money. My shattered pride reflected in my hesitant walk up the few steps to the darkened entrance.

And then I saw him. He was alone at the bar. His Kirk Douglas profile reflected in the shadowed mirror that surrounded the imitation black leather padded bar. How I had dreaded that moment. Dreamt of it in nightmarish fits of sleepless nights.

He saw me and the dimpled smile was there.

"Hi, sit down," he offered.

A restless moment. My eyes shifted like those of a frightened sparrow.

He must not see weakness, I thought.

"How are the kids?" He asked.

I couldn't speak. I just smiled and nodded.

Get over yourself, I ordered my fluttering psyche.

I was in pain, he could tell and merely smiled.

"You look good," he said. But I knew it was insincere flattery. He couldn't fool me anymore.

I smiled back a thank you.

"So," he inquired, "to what do I owe the honor of your visit? Must say it surprised me when you called."

That soft seductive tone I remembered so well. He had the ability to make women melt like butter on a sizzling hot griddle just by the hushed breathless quality in his voice as if you were the one and only. I thought I was the one and only. What a fool.

Staring at him and remembering the pain, I winced and he caught it. So many years together, he read me like a book.

"Look," I said, hoping and praying to be strong I continued, "You must know how tough things are for us, the kids and me, and I need some money, even if it's just enough for food."

I looked into his eyes hoping to see some, even slight glint of compassion or understanding. His eyes were cold and he narrowed them into steely slits and said, "Should have thought about that before you threw me out."

Threw you out? You ran out on us you coward, I thought to myself knowing I had to keep my mouth shut if I were going to get what I needed.

He had more money than God, not only from his job, but also cause he was shacking up with some rich bitch real estate lady in her big ass house in north beach.

I burned up with rage as I thought back to the time when he tried to strangle me after I stuck up for my kids who he tossed around like blond blue-eyed footballs. His thumb closed off my windpipe until I struggled to breathe, my life flashing before my eyes. I fought him for my next breath.

I survived, but knew I should have left then. Yet I sensed at the time that I had to stay because I was so deflated emotionally, so ragged mentally that I felt I had nowhere to go and no one to turn to. Funny thing how it gets you when you are so beaten down that you feel life has no meaning and you only stick it out for the sake of the kids and then he leaves and then what? So, a few horrible but peaceful months passed and, here I was, begging him for support. Ain't life grand?

"Listen Frank," I implored, Christmas is coming up and" … my throat hurt trying not to cry, "Christopher saw this purple banana bike on TV and —"

"Why's that my problem?" he said coldly getting up to leave, "Go find yourself someone else like I did."

Chapter Two

*R*unning out of the bar, crushed, I knew I had to do something to put food on the table, make things a little more bearable for the kids and me. I was determined at that moment not to think of him anymore and focused on filing my divorce. I could hardly afford a divorce but I knew I would find a way if it were the last thing I did.

How the fuck would I pay for that? I wondered. But then I knew the court would eventually force him to pay us child support.

What a dreamer I was.

I couldn't feel the balls of my feet, I had been in line so long. It was so hot and stuffy in that small room I could hardly breathe but I had to do what I had to do. I never thought it would ever get that bad. But there I was the only white woman in the room full of Cubans standing in line for food stamps.

I had no other choice. I kept job hunting but those were tough times for a woman who did not want to be a waitress or a receptionist for practically no money.

A divorced friend of mine down on her luck gave me some tips.

"Dress down." she said, "Accentuate the positive but wear your tightest seediest jeans, grunge it up," she warned, "and add a t-shirt that has seen better days."

I had lots of those.

"Take all the necessary papers, electric bill, mortgage papers and don't forget the tears."

It was embarrassing.

A kind Cuban woman with a warm smile seemed to feel my shame as she looked up at me from her desk.

She asked me about my personal life. I told her I had none.

About my husband. I told her he was shacking up with some broad and that my children needed food.

She asked about my bank account and I began to cry. The tears weren't manufactured. The interview was over.

I qualified for $32.50 in food stamps each month, after approval which would take two weeks. I cried a bit more from anger, frustration and humiliation. She arranged for me to get $32.50 worth of food stamps immediately. I was so happy I cried some more.

$32.50 a month was nice but my mortgage was coming up and if I got another notice about the electric bill or saw my children in another outgrown pair of torn jeans I thought I was going to go out of my mind. I needed cash, a real job and I prayed to God for a miracle.

Chapter Three

"*Y*ou want me to do what?" I asked my mother, Bertha. She gave me one of those looks only a mother could give that put me in my place.

"You heard me, 'Go ask Sammy for a job.' "

Sammy was my brother. A few years before he had some crazy idea of starting up his own bail bonds business and lo and behold! it worked, and he was making a good living over the past year or so. I'd been kind of knocking what he did, knowing very little about the actual business, only that he took people out of jail. The mystery of bail bonds.

I said, it seemed "like a pretty scummy way to make a buck."

And I really did feel that way. As I said, the truth was I didn't even know what the hell a bail bondsman did. Mom had gotten her bail bonds license just six months before. She knew what it was all about. So I asked her.

"By law everyone has the right to be released from jail by a bail bondsman, or other means" My mother explained, "Let's just talk about bondsmen for now, basically, the bondsman puts up whatever money the court decided the bond would be."

She later explained that for the privilege of writing the bond and getting the premium, in other words, his fee, the bondsman would have the right to take collateral to the face value of the bond. It could be property, cash, jewelry or other valuables from the subject that could be turned into cash in case the subject skipped out. This assured the court that the money due would be paid. For that, the bondsmen would get 10 percent of a state bond or 15 percent on a federal bond. The bondsman then becomes 100% responsible for the subject, so if the subject skipped out you could bet your sweet ass the bondsman would hunt him down and bring him to court so he could get his money back. Sounded kind of exciting when she put it that way.

They say pride goeth before a fall but pride was gone and a big fall was sure to come if I didn't get some immediate income. So my mother spoke to Sam and two days later she called me at home and said, "You start Monday morning, be at the office at 10 A.M."

All I could say was, "Yes, Mother."

My brother Sammy was a good talker, flaming red hair and a little on the plump side, he was a wheeler-dealer, a real smooth operator. He needed someone reliable to run his office with my mom and he knew I was a smart cookie and could do it.

Making a regular pay-check was great, but it didn't take long before I saw real money could be made writing the bonds.

"Sammy?" I said one day.

"Yeah?" He answered not really paying attention to me, as usual.

"Let me write that bond, the small one that just came into the office."

He practically laughed in my face. "Lori," all my family called me Lori, "Get real. That's a man's job. Stick to what you're good at."

I was pissed off. He'd sent me to school, sent all of us to school, to get our bonds license.

Who the fuck did he think he was? I knew he loved me a lot, being his only sister and all, but, when it came to the business, well, I *was just a woman, after all.* So, I didn't get to write that bond.

I found out that he was having a hell of time getting one very large bond in particular. It was a grand larceny bond. Shit, about a dozen or so bondsmen were after that little plum – around $25,000. Whoever landed the bond would get 10%, the standard fee for bail bondsmen. $2500 for an hour's work? Not bad, not bad, big money in those days. Lord knows I needed the money so I decided to take my sweet little ass right down to the jail where I knew the guy was interviewing bondsmen. I was well aware that I had something those pigs didn't. It wasn't for sale or rent though, tight dress, big tits and all. Sure enough, I attracted the attention I sought.

The guy looking for the bond, the perp's brother, it turned out, asked me almost laughingly, "You a bondsman?"

"Yes I am." My confidence almost scared me.

His eyes didn't seem to leave my chest, nice, well-rounded breasts in an expensive royal blue silk blouse I went in hock for. And it showed. There's nothing like expensive clothes to hook a guy who knows what he's looking at. I won't lie, I knew he liked what he saw. And I wasn't afraid to dangle the carrot so long as he didn't bite.

I looked at him straight in the eye batting my eyelashes at him playing that dumb blonde role that always served me well and I talked. And I talked and talked, intelligently and you know what? I got the bond. All $25,000 of it. Shocked the shit out of me.

Maybe my body opened the door, but my mind and my ability shipped us in.

I couldn't wait to get back to the office.

"Sammy?"

He sighed, once again not paying me any attention or looking at me, "What Lori? I'm busy."

I slid the paperwork for the bond in front of his face. He looked up, his jaw dropped.

"The perp and his family with the collateral are in the reception room, just check it out Sammy, it's all in order."

"How … how did you?" he stuttered.

I sashayed out the door, "I just stuck to what I was good at."

He smiled. He loved it but had to save his pride.

Many times by sheer will and staying power I got the bond for the office. Sam was impressed, I could tell. I don't know to this day if he really thought I couldn't do it that first time or if that was just a ploy to get me on my toes and fucking well keep me there.

Whatever it was it worked and my bail bonds career took off like a rocket.

Chapter Four

Yeah, Henry was a bastard. A Jamaican lunatic who married Patricia, a good woman with two little girls. They had a son together. Little Henry Jr. was four years old when I met them. I came into their lives when Henry and Patricia were arrested for his sexual abuse of his wife's two young daughters. She was charged with failure to protect.

Leticia was 11, with a light complexion and skinny. Her sister, Janita was 9 years old a chubby, sweet natured little girl. Henry had raped them both continuously over a two year period while Patricia was at night school working towards a nursing degree.

One weekend Leticia went to visit her paternal grandmother, a gentle woman who knew her son did not support his daughter and tried to give her what she could financially and emotionally to try to make up for the lack. She knew that Henry was not a good stepfather but was not prepared for the horror story she heard from her beloved little granddaughter.

Leticia never went home again and a shocked Patricia was called a few days later by the authorities. A short time after that Janita and Henry Junior were removed from the home. Henry Sr. and Patricia were both arrested. Henry stayed in jail for a month while his public defender tried to get his bond reduced. My brother Sam told me to take Patricia out on a $1000 bond and so I did and had full custodial care. So it went.

We felt confident that because Henry couldn't qualify for a bond that Pat and the kids would be secure, or so we thought.

Times were tough. I called her "Pat" and she called me twenty times a day. She moved in with her dad in a little green house on Northwest 79th Street in Liberty City across from a billiards parlor, a noisy bar and a crack house. But the kids were in a safe house over in town, except for Leticia whose grandmother was granted custody. Pat kept going to school and on days when I could I brought her bags of food from Winn Dixie Groceries. Twenty bucks bought a lot of stuff back then, rice and vegetables, hamburger stuff, some coffee, cream and sugar.

Pat also called me "Angel" from "Charlie's Angels", a popular TV series of the day.

"Angel," she said one day when I popped by mid-morning on my way to court, "Got a pot of café Cubano on the stove. Baby, sit down for awhile."

And I did. Café Cubano, mmm … She knew the way to my heart after only a few weeks.

I'd brought her dad some sweet rolls. Poor guy, his body was being consumed by cancer. He sat in his chair by the window all day and watched the world he knew disintegrate before him.

"You here again white girl?" he called to me, his toothless grin and merry eyes belying the agony his body felt.

"Yeah, Slim. I just can't keep away from you, you charming old devil you." I tooted at him.

I went inside and we drank our coffee together. Slim slowly ate a sweet roll, a smile on his face.

The house was in terrible repair, a grim reminder to Slim of just how ill he was. Yet, he was jolly, his black eyes dancing as he joked with me.

"Don't know who's more decrepit me, Sweet Child or this ailing house? Used to be pretty," he said, "When Patty's mama was here. Pink and white flowers all around and a red Bougainvillea bush at the front."

He pointed out the window. His long fingers reaching towards the broken concrete driveway to show me where the Bougainvillea once grew.

"Not there now." He grimaced, "Only broken steps and broken dreams."

I stared at him.

"Papa," Pat encouraged, "Eat your pastry up, Sweet Daddy, before it gets all stale and hard."

She hastily wiped a tear from her eyes. I saw it roll down her cheek.

"Gotta go," I said and rinsed out my cup and headed for the door.

"I'm trying to get a weekend pass for Janita and little Henry to visit with you." I said, "Since you are staying with Pops here it should be okay. Leticia can come too if it's okay with her grandmother."

"That would be great," she said.

"Don't get your hopes up after what happened before I'm not sure I can swing it."

"I remember." Pat said sadly, "Did you know Henry is out?"

"What?" I exclaimed, "When-?"

"The judge reduced the Bond two days ago -"

"Well, forget it, those kids are not coming here. No way. Can't take a chance."

The old man nodded in agreement and in a flash I was in my car that was parked in front of the house and out of there.

I reddened with anger at the thought of Henry being on the loose but with the kids safe and Pat savvy who really cared?

Weeks before the arrests, Henry took Janita and Henry Junior to a hotel on Northwest 79th Street. The jackass checked in using his own name and molested Janita in the hotel. Little Henry Junior saw it all. And he talked.

After the arrests and hoping that I could help build a case against Henry, I used some of my investigative prowess, called in a favor or two and got documented proof that Henry had taken the children to a hotel. Since it was after Leticia's

31

complaint of sexual abuse, he should not have brought them to the hotel. The asshole.

Well, it helped the case against him but I should have known better and almost lost my shiny new bail bonds license as a result. Bail bondsmen are not supposed to overstep certain boundaries like getting classified information from sealed records at hotels. It was very confidential information and the penalties can be severe if the agency that issues bail bonds licenses chooses to enforce the law.

Sam was fit to be tied. However, as it turned out, it was a good thing we knew people in high places, comes in very handy when you do such cavalier stunts. I was well meaning but uninformed, turned out okay though. Things were a bit looser in those days.

Within weeks there was an arraignment for Pat. She pled not guilty, a friend of mine who had his own practice represented her pro bono and got the charges dropped. Her bond was released and I was off the case but we remained good friends.

The reason I was in the court the day that Henry almost killed me with his cane was simply because I hadn't wanted Pat to be there alone. He was going to be sentenced.

So there I was with Pat walking up the courthouse steps. She and the two girls were very apprehensive and I did my best to reassure them.

"So what do you think is going to happen?" Pat asked me, "Will he be found guilty? Will he get life in prison or how many years or will he be found not guilty and –?"

"Hold on." I said. "Pat, relax, the kids don't need this. Let's just calm down and look at things realistically."

We walked over to a stone bench just outside the courtroom at family court and Pat, Leticia, Janita and I sat down.

I put my hand on hers and said as gently as I could, "Don't worry."

Leticia suddenly stood up and ran behind Pat who started to ask her what she was doing, when all four of us looked at the door to the side of the courtroom. Out walked Henry in handcuffs with two uniformed men.

They walked towards the big double doors of the courtroom and as they entered Henry turned, looked at Pat and said very loudly, "See what happens when you trust those white bastards? They broke our marriage up, took our kids and now I'm in jail."

His voice was loud and strident but the guards were holding him back tightly and walked him inside. The little girls were petrified and I took their hands. Pat walked in front as I nodded that we had to go in. We did, and that's when, we saw the uniformed guards release him to the custody of the court bailiffs.

We approached the front of the court and took our places at the bench nearest the judge, and it was at that moment, leaning on his cane that once again he screamed and called out to me.

"You miserable bitch." He said, "It's all your fault."

Without any further words of warning, Henry raised the heavy, carved, wooden cane and tried to bring it down on my head. The two bailiffs grabbed him, throwing him off balance and he fell to the floor. It all happened so fast and in what seemed to be a lightening flash, two more guards moved in and put leg cuffs on him.

Henry would attack no more.

The chagrined judge had had enough and in moments rendered his decision. Henry's sentence was 10 years in prison for his sexual battery and indecent behavior.

"And furthermore," the judge admonished him, "You will keep away from the family and let them live in peace."

He banged the gavel down and left the courtroom.

"It's over." I murmured to Pat and the girls.

"No more, you are safe and dammit so am I. Let's go get a hot fudge Sunday at Howard Johnson."

And we did. Actually, monetarily all I got out of this was less than a hundred bucks but I knew then, I was hooked. I'd been part of a miracle. I realized, at that moment, that more than anything it was my calling to see justice done.

Chapter Five

"Remember, he might have a gun. Put the bastard back in." Sammy said, "He doesn't deserve to be out on the street."

"But –" I started in.

"You wanna learn this fuckin' business, Lori, you better pay attention. You don't know shit. You just got your Goddamn license and if you want to keep it you'd better fuckin' listen to me. He's gonna run. Know what that means? Our money, our *dinero* goes down the toilet – flush, flush. Two thousand bucks. He's over on Southwest 25th Road. Take Hugo and remember he may be armed."

"Okay. Okay." I rolled my eyes.

He always liked to boss me around. But I knew he had good intentions, knew the business inside out and he was sure as hell giving me a chance to make some bucks. As I said before, the business was owned by big ol' Sammy. He was fast becoming the most important man in local bail bonds. He had it topped from South Shore to North Shore and all points in between.

That was a lifetime ago, at a time when little old Miami was not a crime city. A time in the early '70s when "Saturday Night Fever" was still on the eight-tracks, when bell-bottoms were sweeping the sidewalks and platform shoes were all the rage.

Sammy managed to make the bucks though. If a bond was to be written and there was decent money in it, he was there. And little by little he got it all, and it all came alive for me like a Technicolor movie.

Once Sam got used to having me write bonds and saw that if I put my mind to it I could be a real winner, he promised that there would be a lot of money in it for me.

I remember the conversation we had in his office. "Lori, this can be a great business for you, now and in the future if you don't mind taking a few risks here and there.

If I didn't mind taking a few risks?

Well, hell, I never minded taking a chance here and there. Even enjoyed it sometimes, being a Scorpio. Even a little peril was not outside of my frame of reference. Most of all, I knew I would be protected, respected and treated with great regard in that tarnished and polluted -but oh so lucrative-business.

Oh, yeah, I forgot to mention, Sammy is my younger brother. I guess you could say it was more or less a family business since my mother, my youngest brother Brad and Sam's wife were bondsmen, and that was just the beginning of the family legacy. A bona fide dynasty in the making. In years to come, my son as well as Sam's sons would join the ranks.

I decided to try it out for awhile now that I could write my own bonds so I went with Sam and began to write bail bonds. The easy bonds were kind of fun, minimals like traffic and failure to pay child support. Write them up, get the slicker out and get the money. It was just about that easy, like 1-2-3, because bonding in those days was a snap and there was not too much competition. Easy money and, as I soon discovered, a real power trip. Going down to the jail at any hour of the day or night and actually getting in seemed a bit strange and unreal. I knew why I felt that way, because here I was, just little old me. They called me "legs" for a reason. I was a dynamite hot blonde in those days. They said I had tits and ass to last for miles, whatever. I knew what I had and wasn't afraid to keep dangling the carrot if need be.

Getting into the Metro Miami-Dade jailhouse, where all the action was, was easy, with just a flash of my bail bonds license. A high-class soft leather briefcase and my beeper were part of the uniform along with a well-fitting pair of jeans and a soft and casually seductive blouse in the evening, or a classy suit with a short skirt in the daytime. I always favored shades of blue, since they would bring out my eyes and God knows, a gal going into the jail back in those days needed all the help she could get.

It was still a man's world in the bail bond business. But it would not be that way forever.

Getting past the duty officers at the jail was a good part of the fun. There were always a few cute remarks and some come - hither glances, a smile here and there as I negotiated with the guards and made my way into the inner sanctum that was the Miami-Dade County jail. Then it was off to meet the subject in jail. I would enter into the hallowed territory reserved for bondsmen and attorneys deep in the hidden recesses of the Metro Justice Building. Imagine this, it was like walking into a mysterious tunnel. With the harsh glare of fluorescent lighting of the jail's hallway all but blinding me, I'd refocus and look inside the cell straight into the eyes of a person who was arrested only a few hours ago.

Very interesting how we bondsmen would get to see only their eyes. Took me awhile to figure out how the jail officers managed to always have the prisoners at a height that would allow only their eyes to be visible from outside the cell. The light finally dawned on me one day as to how this masterful, ingenious plan was accomplished, and with verification from one of the guards, I found it was true. They had little wooden stepstools in varying heights and the guards would find and use the one that would allow only eye contact with the visitor. A simple but very effective idea that almost always worked. After all, it was not really necessary to see the size and shape of them. Who the hell cared? The important thing was to look into their eyes, where the clandestine pools of their souls were floating in brilliant blue or smoky hazel or smoldering, shadowy black. That was an important clue. We bondsmen soon learned to look into those eyes and seek out truth or lies. Most of the time our gut instincts were right. We weren't friggin' psychics, but trusting that primordial, primitive piece of gray matter resting in our skulls sometimes colorfully referred to as the alligator brain - usually saw us through.

Yes, we saw only their eyes until such time as we bonded them out AND marched them out of the jail, and then their full glory was revealed to us. Most of the time it was not too glorious. But it was ever fascinating. It's really important to our business to understand that eyes tell a story all their own, sometimes the truth, sometime an obvious, obsidian black lie. But sometimes, only sometimes, a sad innocence comes across. Those are the dangerous times, when our sympathy might override our good judgment and cost us money, lots of money, and we can end up on the other side of nowhere. Often there is a kind of flat indifference, almost apathy, thinly, though cleverly disguised and discernable only to the proficient eyes of skilled professionals, be they attorneys, investigators or bail bondsmen. And it's true that since we are not privy on the first meeting to seeing their entire bodies, and the language they reflect, it is next to impossible to use our understanding of body language to interpret their intentions. So we had to learn to read those eyes.

And we did. Sometimes we won and sometimes we lost. Thanks to who knows what, we won most of the time, so we stayed in business. I never really thought of it as a business. It was more like a fun and games challenge. But once we got to see with whom we would be dealing, it became discussion time and the incarcerated gal or fellow would almost always start off with:

"I don't know why I'm here, I didn't do nothing."

Of course, you "didn't do nothing," asshole, that's why I'm here, and that's why it's gonna cost you. I never said it. A smile would suffice.

Then we'd get down to the business at hand. The most important parts first. Money. Who cared about anything else relating to this little adventure? Did you think it was our altruistic natures that had us trotting down to the jail to help these poor pitiful souls get out of a lock-up that they were convinced they didn't deserve? No, it was business, pure business that motivated us.

I was catching on real fast. Usually the bond would be qualified by a secretary or one of the bondsmen in the office. That meant that the "perp," our terminology for any person behind bars who had a few bucks, or was able to get someone to guarantee with cash or property that he or she would appear in court at the appointed time and not run off or "skip" as we like to say, had been found more or less acceptable. That was a major "golden rule" of bonding. Get it in writing and in the bank or in the vault and then negotiate to put their feet on the street. However, many people that were arrested lived by their own "golden rules" and they were usually neither golden nor rules. According to the perp, he or she would never skip, God forbid. That was the other poor bastard who did that.

Yeah, well, I knew that, but it was just a precaution. It was the procedure we followed to cover our asses.

I was learning the business and earning money. So life was good, real good. I worked part-time some days and in the same office along with my mother, sister-in-law and youngest brother, Brad.

It was a business all right, but I never realized how dirty or low-down it could be.

Chapter Six

 $\mathcal{I}$ t never failed to amaze me what sick bastards you can come across in a bail bonds office. One day when everyone was at court for one thing or another, Sam beeped me early and asked me to open the office. He asked me to go in about 9 o'clock and do the usual morning routine - check messages, make coffee, and wait for his trusty, Tommy, to come to the office and go through the mail. Having nothing really pressing to do since the kids were in school, I hopped in my old Toyota and was on my way.

Going to the office was a diversion and in a lot of ways better than going off to the jail at all hours of the day or night. So Sam called me many mornings to cover for our mother or whoever was not coming in that day. Although the office was only about half a mile from my house on Alton Road, Miami Beach, I would first have to go into the city of Miami to get the mail. God only knows why Sammy insisted on having our mail drop in Miami although there were several post offices near us, but he had his own reasons. Perhaps it was because his very first office had been in Miami several years before and it was just easier to keep paying on the old box rather than seeking out a new one.

Sam had gotten a good deal on a converted office building on the Beach a few months before, an old three bedroom Art Deco type building located just a block away from the Miami Beach Police. Prime spot, low money. Sam's lucky day.

The ride over the Julia Tuttle Causeway always thrilled me. All that blue sky and water and the warm, soft tropical early morning wispy clouds billowing over on gentle wind currents across beautiful Biscayne Bay made me really happy to be alive. I have always loved the steamy, hot, humid and sometimes misty mornings that we have in South Florida. Usually by midday it's hotter than hell must be, the early morning cool replaced by a stifling stillness in the air, saved only by the blessed ocean breeze that wafts over from the beach. And so it goes until the sun sinks into the western sky and the blazing heat releases its grip on the city.

I got to the post office in record time and when I pulled up at the office, there in the driveway in his red pickup truck was Tommy, our mail boy. He was not exactly a boy. He was about 30, blond hair, tall and wiry, sort of a trailer park mentality. Sam had taken him out of jail and, fascinated by his story, had helped him to get trusty status and work around our

43

office. His original crime was not too serious, but by our standards in those days, it was horrendous.

He had been convicted of bilking and defrauding about three dozen people out of nice fat down payments on a nonexistent health club. This was the '70s, and we were not quite as sophisticated about health clubs as we later became. But that was not what made Tom special. What really gave him star status was his brother. You remember the guy who shot and crippled the old governor from Georgia? Well, that was his brother. It was front-page stuff for weeks and dear old big brother was in the federal slammer in Georgia when little brother decided on a life of minor crime. Sam to the rescue, and Tommy was now installed as a regular fixture at the bail bonds office. His brother's notoriety and celebrity status brought us business.

Sam was really clever about picking up help from the jail. Lots of folks had trades. Some were plumbers and bricklayers, even electricians. They got their fannies jammed in the slammer from time to time for some petty infraction of the law or larcenous criminal activity, but they usually turned out to be cooperative, appreciative and real cheap help for Sam. Right from the beginning, I was never crazy about taking some of these creeps out of jail and bringing them to the office to work, as most of the time they were really sleazy and I truly felt they belonged in jail.

In the sick, cut-throat "who's going to put the perp's feet on the street" world of bail bondsmen it usually comes down to who's got some star slam, some shine. In that case, the bail bonding business becomes a real happening to prospective customers.

But in our criminal justice system everyone is given the right to bail, save for a few serious crimes, like homicide or sexual battery, and the overworked public defenders were always out there seeking some sort of probationary escape for their charges. Bondsmen and attorneys had first crack at the "talents" of these men, and sometimes women, and more than once really got burned.

Greed was not a noun, a verb nor any other part of speech in this business. It was a fact of life.

We had never had any problems with Tommy, found him to have a very Southern, congenial way, with a hint of gentility, perhaps a little decadence, and certainly lots of good old boy charm. Upon closer scrutiny he was slow-talking and shifty-eyed. His eyes never moved above my chest.

I went into the office with Tom close behind and suffered the usual morning chores of opening blinds, running water for coffee and taking the phones off service. The mail he carried in for me was deposited on the reception desk for a quick look-over, usually by whoever felt like looking at it, at least until Sam came in. On that particular day it was my turn to see what bills and checks had come in, and I decided to do it immediately. I did that in case Sam called in early, as he was sometimes apt to do, if the first call bond hearings were over very quickly due to the judge not being there or fewer people being jailed the night before.

Yes indeed, the whole thing depended on who was arrested, when and for what. The way the bond hearing works is that all people arrested the day or night before would be brought into the courtroom very early in the morning to appear before a judge for what is called the IA or initial appearance.

The judge would listen to what the arresting officers had to say and their recommendation regarding bail. Then based on what he heard, and banking on his legal knowledge and experience, and taking a close look at the arrestee, the judge would make a determination.

Bail bondsmen were all over the courthouse hoping for a bond release to help pay their rent. Most of the bondsmen located their offices as close to the courthouse as they possibly could. This made for a very desirable although somewhat seedy neighborhood, and the rents were enormously high. But be that as it may, they were high-priority rentals, and it was a cut-throat situation even way back then when one became available. The other type of judge-ordered release from jail is a special release called ROR (release on own recognizance) if the judge felt you were responsible and credible and trustworthy, you could be released knowing, or at least hoping, that you wouldn't skip bail. That was supposed to be, and usually was, used on persons who were upstanding citizens and got caught up with some minor infraction of the law, and it was undoubtedly their first offense.

The paperwork would indicate that the person would promise to appear in court for an arraignment and any pretrial conferences and would be notified directly by the court.

The recidivism or repeat offense rate was high on ROR and only the court was responsible for finding the offender if he failed to show up for the court dates. On the other hand, if the judge decided on a bond, and only he could determine the amount, a whole different set of rules went into effect. The arrested person would be returned to the jail and then a bondsman would go to see him and work out the details of his release. It was quite interesting to see just how the arrested person would find a bondsman.

Sometimes his or her parents or friends would know one or would know someone who knew a bondsman and then one phone call would set the whole process in motion. Sometimes the arrested person would simply look up at a large black felt board posted inside the jail. On it in little white plastic letters were the names of all the bail bondsmen in the area and all the arrested person had to do was select a name and make a collect call from the nearby pay telephone.

In lots of situations, in those wild and wooly early days, the bondsmen, hungry for new clients, would simply hang out and solicit the folks in the waiting room who were obviously relatives or friends of detainees and who could throw the bonds their way. Jail officials frowned on this practice, but it was done anyway. Actually, on the way in that morning, I was passing by the jail on my way to have a quickie breakfast and I thought I'd stop in just to have a fast look-see as to what was going on and who was there hunting for bonds. A guy came up to me as I entered the room and asked the usual question after I got the usual up and down look. You'd think these jerks had never seen a nice pair of legs or spectacular boobs.

So, I looked at him like I was smelling a fart, smiled sweetly and said, "Oh yes, sir I am a bondsman. Do you need a bond written?"

"Well," he replied, stroking his wispy little gray beard, I guess I do, is there some place we can go for a cup of coffee and talk about it"

No, fuck you, pal, I thought. Thought better of it and turned on my lovely high heel and walked out. Discretion *is* the better part of valor when you have to make a living, and I learned long ago how to keep my mouth shut when necessary.

No matter how it came about, a bondsman would eventually be called, the bond qualified, and a bondsman from the office would go down and actually write the bond and put the perp's feet on the street. Actually, we required that people who put up collateral go back to our office and fill out a lot of paperwork designed to protect them from the possible loss of their collateral. But, more important, protect *us* against a possible skip by the client we helped get out of jail. There is something about having the family jewels or the mortgage to your mother's house signed over and locked up in a bondsman's safe that tends to keep things on the up and up. Smart bondsmen insisted on collateral for the full face value of the bond, knowing very well that it would be really terrible if the client skipped and the collateral was short. It could and did put some bondsmen out of business really fast. Cruel as it may sound, it's pretty much exactly what happened.

Imagine having to pay the court $50,000 to $100,000 out of your own pocket. That would occur because you were not holding enough of the money so you had to use your own money to pay the court if someone skipped out on a bond.

Back at the office, I sat down at the desk, the front desk they called it in those days, a kneehole desk, with a flat top and two rows of drawers on either side. Sitting down, my knees fit quite comfortably between the two rows of drawers. Tom went into an adjoining office and hollered out that he was going to get himself a nice, hot cup of coffee. As I busied myself with work, I never noticed that his dreamy southern drawl had suddenly gone very quiet. I called out, "Say, Tom, where's the happy talk?"

At that moment somebody under the desk grabbed my left foot, removed my shoe and began sucking on my toes. Good God. It was Tom. He'd come in without my noticing what was happening. What kind of corrupted being did we have here in the office, alone with me and my foot?

I tried to kick him and pulled his hair and I was trying to pull my foot out of his mouth while screaming, "Stop it, you nut, you perverted fool." I realized that this creep was really strong and without any doubt experienced at this sort of exploitation since he was holding on fast and tight. After another harrowing few seconds passed, he released my foot and stuck his head up over my desk from his squatting position, flashing me a stupid grin.

"You pervert," I screeched again," much louder this time, hoping to unnerve him. "I've read about your kind in magazines. Get up from there and get away from me!"

In spite of my protest and obvious contempt of his disgusting habit, he still had an asinine look on his face. He dived under the desk and grabbed my other foot and de-shoed it. Well, that was too much! I grabbed for the telephone and called my mother, who was at home.

Let me tell you a little about my mother, Bertha. First of all, she hated the name Bertha and so everyone called her Bert. Something about some artillery gun in World War I called "Big Bertha" kind of put her off. Oh well, what's in a name? Mom was also working at the office, most of the time as a part-time secretary and part-time bail bondsman. In those early days, pre-women's lib, no one would have ever been called a bondswoman. "Bondslady" certainly did not wear well. Write the bonds, get the collateral and the fee; who the hell cared what we were called? Most assuredly, not my mama.

So I said to her "Mom, Tommy, our irreverent mail boy is under my desk, and the son of a bitch has my foot in his mouth, and he won't let go."

She laughed and said, "Put the jerk on the phone." So I dragged the receiver over the top of the desk and told him to speak to my mother.

He did. And all I heard was, "But gee, Bert, I'm only sucking on one little toe of Lori's, I'm not hurting her," pause, "Well 'cause I like her feet, 'cause I like feet."

That was enough for me. In one double-barreled move, I yanked the phone from his ear and my foot from his mouth and shrieked that if he didn't get out of the office, I would call Sam in court. He got out of the office, my mom called back and Sam called on line two, all in the next 30 seconds. Sam spoke to Tom for just a minute or two, but his smile disappeared instantly and he walked slowly from the office with his head slightly bowed. The old Southern charm had melted like butter on a nice hot piece of cornbread fresh out of the oven.

After that I wore only heavily laced tennis shoes to work, never knowing if Old Toe Sucking Tom would be on the job. But I didn't mind that much. I was a girl who could take care of myself, and besides I needed the job. With two kids to support, it wasn't easy for me in those days.

Bail bondsmen are a strange lot. They are living in a carnival atmosphere, and Tommy was carnie all the way.

In the months to come, we discovered Tom had a penchant for more than female toes. We kept him around because he was worth more than the trouble he caused. Sometimes late at night one of the bondsmen would bring a prisoner out of jail and take him directly to the office until the collateral arrangements were completed and receipts made out and all the paperwork complete. This, on nights when there was heavy bonding out, meant that the office would be like a Ringling Brothers Circus until all hours.

Naturally, Tom would be running around like the proverbial chicken carrying out Sam's orders and keeping the populace of the office happy in general. One night he got more specific and at 5 a.m. when Sam and Terry, his sometimes partner, returned to the office, Tom was naked, mounted astride a lovely young thing who had been arrested for, of all things, solicitation to commit prostitution. Imagine!

Sam was furious and Tommy ran, without his pants, into the bleakness of a cool Miami night and earned himself yet another title. He was henceforth referred to as "saddle-up" Tom. Just another busy night at All the Best Bail Bonds.

My other brother Andrew had already graduated and gone into business law. He first went to New York, but then decided that he would love to live in San Francisco, where he opened a practice and became very successful. Over the years, we all went out to visit with him and his wonderful wife, Meg, and when Mom got fed up with Miami Beach, she went out west to stay with Andrew and Meg. But her heart was really and truly nestled in our tropical clime, and after the first big earthquake scared the crap out of her, she returned to Miami Beach, nevermore to leave.

We all adored our mother and she played a very important part in our lives. She never married again, telling me that she was totally fulfilled with her kids, her work and her friends, of which she had many. After her return to Miami, she spent years working at an armed forces base in a civilian capacity, and eventually rose to the highest level possible. But more than anything else, she loved working with Sammy in the bail bonds business, and helped him in the early days to build it up to the big success that it remains to this very day.

I've gotta tell you, some of Sam's associates were real sleaze bags, including a lot of the so-called respected attorneys who were on the prowl back then for an easy good time. I must have been very naïve because it surprised the hell out of me.

Why, one of them, sick bastard that he was, loved the ladies all right, the little ladies - little, little ladies. After 10 or 11 they got too tall for him. And probably too smart. Boy, did I ever get a shock to see and hear for myself the truth about this guy. In all fairness he was not one of Sam's good buddies or goombahs. No, just a run-of-the-mill criminal attorney with three other partners and a diseased mind. He had a very nice wife at the time who was about 26. A little too old for him, we soon came to realize. Sick bastard that he was.

There was a favorite spot where we all kind of hung out, a late night bistro way up on Biscayne Boulevard, sort of a 1920's style joint, open until the wee hours. I really should say the "*whee*" hours - it was that kind of place. A drop-in kind of eatery where you could always get a good steak or a piece of Key lime pie. Nothing formal, but real pretty, like an old speakeasy. Matter of fact, that's what they called the place, the Speakeasy.

It was supposedly a hangout for whatever mob was in town. In those days it was simple. No Latino bad guys, no Haitian scaries like there were after the 80's. No, just a few wise guys with kind of flat noses and tightly closed lips, who wore dark glasses at night and expensive gabardine suits with silk shirts. They never bothered anyone, kept to themselves, and took in every action that was going down in the joint.

Being a bondsman gave me a lot of leeway. I could sort of freewheel myself into places that a lady would never care or even dare to go. Or if they did care to, they'd be looked at kind of funny. But, me, I could pop up anytime, almost anywhere and never get much of the big eye. And boy, could I listen. My brain was a natural tape recorder.

This one particular night, I had just finished writing a late bond and was kind of antsy for a little male company. The kind of guys who would know better than to try and jump my bones. I felt secure because the kids were asleep, and going home to a lonely house was not on my agenda. I stopped off at a little Cuban all-night spot on Southwest Eighth Street (long before it came to be called Calle Ocho), and had a colada, my favorite. A unique blend of Cuban coffee and sugar that has enough caffeine in it to resurrect the dead. It was a real treat and usually had enough caloric value to keep me from being hungry, but not that night.

I could usually pick up a little newsy chit-chat about what was going on in town - certainly more to see and hear at these little "cafecitos" than there was in the morning newspapers, especially about the Latin citizenry. Matter of fact, much of what we heard in that place turned up a couple of days later, as a news flash on TV or in the Miami Herald.

But tonight there was not much going on. I had my fix, my cup of café Cubano, and it was raining like hell and I was still feeling hungry. I also just didn't feel like driving home yet, so I decided to head for the Speakeasy where I could always depend on a good Caesar salad and a steak. I ordered a Cuba Libre, another marvelous Cuban concoction made of smooth golden rum and Coca Cola.

Like I said, that at one time the mob called the Speakeasy, home. Actually, from all my encounters there, I think they still did, in a quiet sort of way. No hell raising, no shootouts and in the back room ... but that's another story. And it made sense that a really dark, cozy little joint that had all of the characteristics that identify such places as the mob joints we have read about, seen on television or in the movies, would be one. Play the game, wear the name. Fancy, dark red velvet drapes, crystal chandeliers and lots of gold looking goodies placed around the room.

Even the waitresses looked kind of goldy in their skin tight gold leotards and blond pony tails swishing this way and that as they walked on their Playboy

Bunny high heels moving all their parts and leaving little to the imagination. But in spite of all the liquid sexuality floating around, there was always a considered air of respectability about the place. No messing around here, or Nino, the old Italian owner of the place who missed nothing, nada, ever, would see a problem happening, and then, out you'd go.

Shorty, the depraved lawyer I mentioned before, was at the bar when I got there. I sat down at a table pretty close to the bar and certainly didn't have to strain my sweet little ears for this one. He was talking a mile a minute to an assorted group of lawyers and other professionals, some of whom I recognized. The looks on their faces varied from smiles to utter disbelief.

"You should see this," he chirped out, "she's only twelve, but, you'd think she was fourteen. And boy is she hot, she made my little dickie bird whistle."

Could I believe my ears, he said a 12 year-old?

Then the sicko went on. "And her mother, she knows what a pistol she's got on her hands, truth is she ain't much taller, and she calls me over and tells me what a handful she is and could I think of some way to tame her down a bit. Could I? You bet. The old lady and I sort of made a deal. She even told me I could take pictures as long as her husband didn't find out."

He stopped talking as he saw me get up. That was enough for me, more than enough.

As I walked over to Mr. Perversion, my flesh was crawling and my mind was flashing like a

56

spinning kaleidoscope on what I would do or say. But something took over and without another thought I threw my rum and coke, my delicious Cuba Libre, in his sweaty, horrible little face.

Up until that moment he didn't know who I was. I thought he saw me when I sat down, but realized at that moment that he really had not recognized me. So we had a few choice words ending with "and maybe the Miami Herald would like to know a little of what I heard tonight." I was soon to find out that I ended Sam's lucrative bond association with that bucket of crap that night.

"Sorry," I explained after I got home later that night to brother Sammy on the phone, "but, I couldn't help it."

He said, "Talk to you tomorrow," and hung up.

Moments like this gave me pause as to what the hell I was doing in this business. Was he the lawyer or the perp? It was a dangerous game I was playing late at night out there on the streets of Miami alone. But I loved it, the challenge, the possible danger. I was seeing the seamy side for the first time in my life and unafraid, I lapped it up like a kitten with a bowl of sweet, warm milk.

But I knew I was no kitten. Even with the little exposure I had to the mean streets, I felt that this- or at least some form of criminology was my cup of tea.

I wasn't fearful of dealing with the seamier side of humanity. Careful yes, and I'd learn to be even more careful as time went on. It's called staying alive and I was very much into doing that. Years later some Pollyanna-type editor would refer to me as "a bit hardboiled". Yeah, lady, well I have little interest in French bedroom furniture too.

Chapter Seven

*N*ot all the guys I met in the bonding game were bastards. There was Don Wentworth, for example. He and Sam had been partners, opening their first bail bond business together long before I ever thought about becoming a bondsman. But Don was not really serious about the business and had his fingers in too many other pies. And I knew his life story, growing up on the Beach with no dad, a mom who ran a bar down on South Beach and was never home.

Don had more meals at our house when he was a kid than he ever had at home. He'd show up about suppertime three, four nights every week. We always had enough. When either my mother or I cooked, we cooked up enough for an army. With three brothers, all a little bit younger than I, there were always lots of young guys hanging around who looked like they needed a good meal. And Don was the neediest of all. He tried teaming up with Paul Langley as a PI for awhile, then moved on to some other kind of shady associations. We all remained good friends and Don was always a gentleman to me.

One day, when my daughter, Allison, was very young and I was still married to her piece of shit drunkard dad, Frank, I was doing some shopping on Washington Avenue with her in the carriage when a couple of toughs came up to me, surrounded me and asked for money. My first instinct was to protect Allison, and as I moved toward her, one of the guys grabbed me.

In one second flat I heard, "Let go of her, or I'll kill you," and up loomed Don Wentworth and banged their heads together in a most incredible show of brute force and consummate strength.

"Gee, thanks, Don," I stammered, more or less in shock. Actually, I don't know what I'd have done if he hadn't shown up at that moment. He just shrugged it off with, "Maybe you ought to have something to carry around to protect yourself."

I knew what he meant, but the thought of a gun in my baby's carriage was horrifying. Nowadays it's almost part of my dress code and as essential to my well-being as my lipstick or mascara.

I still walked on Washington Avenue almost every day, and I loved to shop there at the Butterflake Bakery. We devoured lots and lots of black and white cookies, the very best on the Beach. We shopped for food at Thrifty Super Market and enjoyed matinees at the old Paris Theatre until they started showing dirty movies. South Beach at that time was full of old folks. The joke going around for years was that old people lived in Miami Beach and their parents lived in St. Pete.

How things change. I often think back to my rough, tough, but kindly friend Don Wentworth, and how a gun eventually changed his life forever. But that was years later. And a few years after that, out of necessity, a gun did become an integral part of my wardrobe. At one time I thought about opening a school to teach women to shoot and not be fearful of guns since we were right in the midst of the Wild-West '70s in Miami Beach. It would have worked but I was learning a profession from the ground up, so the timing was off.

I wanted to call the school the "Powder Puff Academy," hire off-duty cops, real lookers, to handle the ladies, decorate the place in pink lacy stuff and advertise the hell out of it. No one else has ever done it, so perhaps one day I'll look into the possibility again. Pink bullets? But I was too busy then and it sort of drifted away from me.

Life was changing for me. I had to get divorced at that time and in the early '70s women of my age had a hard time divorcing and supporting their children, and even though I made a decent living, the stress and strain of domestic problems were taking their toll on me.

Not that I didn't love the guy, you understand. He was handsome and sexy, a great lover, unfortunately to a lot of other women as well as me, which, oddly, made him very exciting. Of course, what's exciting at 19 is looked at a little differently at 25. Particularly when one has, as I do, the personality and makeup of a one and only. Yep, I have to be the one-and-only, the be-all and the end-all, or else it isn't worth it.

We drifted back and forth with our marriage like that for a good number of years. If he didn't drink and came home before midnight and I was a good girl, then our reconstruction period, like after the Civil War, would jump into gear. Then oops, something, and off he'd go drinking again for a week or two. And then it would be sheer hell. I still shudder at the memory.

Talk about a roller coaster - this was the fastest, highest ride around. And I was living on it. Pretty soon, because of the kids, I decided to put an end to it all. He was a great believer in domestic violence, and it came time to draw the line. In today's world the bastard would have been wearing gray and living with three hots and a cot in a heartbeat. We used that slang a few years ago to explain three hot meals and a bed in a jail cell. Sounds so much like today. I was really ashamed of the abuse I suffered, and being the private person I am, kept it very much to myself. My brothers never knew. I became very adept at covering up my black eyes.

So off he went, and I enjoyed my newfound privacy and lack of fear of having myself and the kids kicked around like a bunch of blue-eyed blond footballs. My marriage was over. Frank, the bastard was shacking up with some real estate bitch in North Miami. Hardly ever came home to see one of the kids. And what was more, the last time I saw him he threatened to kill me. Most of my evenings, when I was not writing bonds, saw me happily at home with Allison and Chris. I was very sad and lonely, but don't think for an instant that I was alone too long.

He had to be the sexiest man I'd seen in a long time. His name was Jim Dawson, nice guy, health nut, rode a bicycle, had a bug-eyed sprite Alpha Romeo and worked as a cabana manager at one of the oceanfront hotels. He was great with my kids and as you can probably tell, that was paramount with me. He would joke with them about eating yogurt, which my son, Chris, found disgusting.

Jim would tease him with, "You will eat the strawberry yogurt, you will like it and you will ask for more." The kids got a real kick out of Jim's humor and I really appreciated him for lightening things up a lot. We had a nice little something going. As a matter of fact, we did even in the last seamy, sordid days of my horror-story marriage. Discreetly, of course, but it kept me together enough to do what needed doing and gave me a safe harbor - so to speak - over at the beach. I was never ashamed of my doings. I deserved a little happiness and who on God's earth would ever point the finger at me after all I'd been through?

They say ignorance is bliss, but what is there to say about total stupidity? Jim had a clever cover and no one would ever suspect that this generous man, father of a little boy and divorced from a woman he described as a raging lunatic, would ever do anything to jeopardize a relationship with me, whom he called the most marvelous woman in the world. As a matter of fact, come to think of it, he called me Beauty. Who would ever think? Well, think again. Jim lived a rather odd life as the single parent of a delightful 7-year-old boy. They lived in two cabanas at the oceanfront hotel where he worked, complete with a shower, two double beds and the amenities the hotel cabanas provided, like a telephone. So when I finally took my kids and went home, we could talk all night. And there was lots to talk about. He was building a sailboat, a very large one, a 65-footer, designed as a Boston Whaler, and we were going to sail far away to the other side of the world with our three kids and live out all of our fantasies.

We spoke endlessly of our dreams of sailing all the oceans, going all around the world. I was even collecting books to home-school the children so they would become world-traveled little geniuses. Who could know what was coming?

One wonderful moonlit night Jim and I were sitting outside the cabana where he and Oliver slept and he said to me "Beauty, next year at this time we'll have traveled over thousands of sea miles with our kids and visited dozens of exotic ports, we'll have dined in foreign lands on glorious foods and have memories to last us at least the rest of our lives. The kids will be so well educated by seeing life for real, not just learning about it in a classroom"

I said, "Oh Jim you are such a romantic dreamer can't you ever see any of the negatives or hardships we may have to endure and we'll never see our families and--"

I choked up at that moment, but with a hard look on his face and a firm set to his jaw, he said, 'that'll be no loss- at least not for me."

That was the first time I had ever heard him speak that way and it scared me a little bit. But locked tightly in the euphoria of the moment, in the fantasy of traveling the globe, I chose not to give it any import. I should have.

We were able to eat most of our meals at the hotel's coffee shop, which was a stone's throw from the cabana, as was the pool, and of course the glorious ocean for late night swims. It was idyllic. Whenever I had some free time, I'd trot over there after work, and the kids would come over after school, and the three of them would play together until dinnertime. Then we'd either barbecue steaks or hot dogs in front of the cabana or go out to eat, usually in the coffee shop at the hotel. But sometimes we would get all dressed up and Jim would take us to a fancy restaurant. He made lots of money and spent it freely on my kids and me.

Oliver, his little son, was a joy, musically talented and already playing the violin. Tall for his age, he talked all the time about becoming a famous basketball player. To be an All Star, that was what he wanted. He did indeed become famous years later, but as a movie star. Oliver adored my two and thought of them as his slightly older brother and sister. My cousin Rick, who was Allison's age, often spent weekends with us, and he too enjoyed the sand and the surf and all the love we shared.

The nature of Jim's work afforded him the privilege of keeping his son near him. And those were glorious days on the beach for all of us. That is until one day when Allison confided something to me.

"Mom", she said to me, "I gotta tell you something, its kinda bad, I think and" she stopped for a minute and I could see she was struggling to find the right words. Then she went on slowly. "Well, you see, Oliver told us that Jim touched him *there,* you know what I mean mom, and he did it all the time and he put his mouth there and oh God,"

I was in shock, me, who thought she'd seen and heard it all finding out in the most gruesome way that my lover, the man I felt I could trust *was nothing more than a fuckin' pedophile.* Oh, there was more, much more. I didn't want to believe it, but it became more and more evident Oliver was telling the truth. The brutal truth was out and there was no going back, but until we all actually believed him, Oliver was put through the torture of re-living the incidents again and again. We finally took him to see a very well-known child psychologist.

Jim vehemently denied it all, but Oliver knew too much and was graphically correct in his descriptions of his sexual abuse. At one point Jim tried to tell me that perhaps Oliver had spied on us during a moment of high passion, but I didn't buy it. It was all true. Oliver was the victim of a seriously sick deviate father who performed oral sex on this little boy. I really knew how to friggin' pick 'em.

So much for what I thought would be the great romance of my life. It was over.

Jim and Oliver rode off in Jim's little green bug-eyed sprite Alpha Romeo to parts unknown. Today that sort of perversion, when brought to light, carries severe penalties, like perhaps a lifetime prison sentence, but at that time the only penalties paid, unfortunately, were by the victim or victims as it turned out to be.

It was a tremendous blow to my psyche, discovering that the man I cared for, who made love to me with such passionate intensity, was involved in the heinous depravities of an incestuous relationship with his 7-year-old son.

God, I can remember feeling so depressed, downtrodden, useless, despondent and dejected. In fact, there were not enough adjectives to describe my feelings, no depths low enough for my tortured heart to find rest and ease. Besides feeling dreadfully sorry for myself, which under the circumstances would be quite normal, I was filled with the guilt that I had not seen anything wrong.

The abuse had been going on for some time, at least for a year or so, apparently, and little Oliver was afraid to tell anyone until it just became too much for him. My every thought was for this child. I was obsessed with anger and the frustration that there was nothing I could do to take Oliver away from this very abusive situation. It was not within my rights.

Jim was the father. In today's world it would be quite another matter, but I was his lover, without much credibility. And along with the guilt and despair, I was embarrassed as hell because some of my friends found out about the situation. I felt that my privacy had been completely invaded. To everyone on the outside it looked really awful and I seemed the fool.

I knew deep in my soul that I would come through this indignity, pick up remnants of my life, as I had before, and move on. I knew this in my heart because I wasn't a quitter, had no use for what I considered to be weakness of spirit. Then again, there were my two kids who, although they did not comprehend the enormity of the situation, were still dramatically affected and needed my care and consolation.

My daughter Allison knew exactly what was going on, she being a mature 12-year-old at the time, and the others, my son, Chris, and cousin Rick, younger though they were, felt the uneasiness and tension.

Many years, later when my life was more settled and I was following my real calling in life, a wonderful man I worked for, whose name is well known in Washington, told me that to survive was nothing - cockroaches had survived for 50 million years, and so what? To prevail was all.

I didn't know that then, not about the roaches, or prevailing, but I would soldier on.

After Jim left town, I was very sad in spite of myself, cried a lot, nursed my wounds and got my life back together.

Chapter Eight

*N*ext up at bat in the great baseball game called life was a lusty fellow from England, handsome, sexy and full of the joy of life, or at least it seemed so at that time. It was contagious, and after my rueful recent love affair, my melancholy heart took hold of the joy and began to heal.

Jack was his name, I met him at a show where he was performing and we really hit it off. He was a sexy son of a bitch, and I was ready for some hot sex and possibly some real love. Whatever that was. Interesting guy, he told me all about my life from an astrological point of view. And no, no etchings for this bright boy. He painted his love for me on a canvas filled with my Scorpio sun, my Aquarian moon, and my Leo ascendant. I was very leery after the scumbag I had just been involved with. I knew that Jack's little Pisces heart had been wounded by the selfish meandering of his callous former wife.

He was fascinated by the fact that I was a bail bondsman and said that I was perfectly suited astrologically for that type of work.

Jack and I saw each other very often because he was singing in Miami Beach and I was leading a wonderfully single life and had all the time in the world, when I wasn't working, to devote to him and our new relationship. There was no need to worry about my children because months before, when my divorce turned nasty, I had sent them to live temporarily in San Francisco, with my brother Andrew and his wife, Meg.

So once again I sought the great romantic adventure of my life. And I found it. Jack and I loved the same things, great food, sex, walks on the beach, sex, songs from the 50's and sex. How could we fail?

Jack came over to the house one night about a month after we met and said to me,

" I did your horoscope and we are perfect for each other"

"How romantic", I replied.

"No, seriously, your moon is in Aquarius and my Venus is in Aquarius, and that is the positioning of true lovers. Remember the words from the song "Aquarius"?

And he sang to me in that deep, wonderful voice, "When the moon is in the 7th house and Jupiter aligns with Mars, well, your moon *IS* in the 7th house and your Jupiter is aligned with Mars so combining that with your Scorpio water sign sun and my Pisces water sign sun and the fact that we both have Leo risings, we cannot fail."

I just smiled, what the hell could I say?

He went on, "but apart from astrology, I love the way you are, so beautiful, so nice to be with, you make my life happy just to be near you and I remember the first time we met and I never believed in love at first sight until then. You looked so vulnerable and so honest and so gorgeous in that plain black velvet dress and I'm happy that you went to the club that night and I found you."

Jack stopped talking and took me in his arms and kissed me very tenderly. I was so afraid to love and trust him after all that I'd been through, but I knew at that moment that my searching days were over. And so were his. We were inseparable after that.

As soon as my divorce became final, I was able to bring Allison and Chris back from San Francisco to their home in Miami Beach. They were glad to be home but a bit stand-offish about Jack at first, and he wisely kept his distance for the first month.

As they say, hindsight is 20/20. Well, as I said, in the great baseball game of life, we were at second base and headed for a home run before I even stopped to take a breath. And my kids really got used to Jack, this Englishman who took Chris fishing and told Allison to wash the dishes, to her utter and complete chagrin. But, she did it anyway. What was lacking in our life, apart from a little happiness, was a little discipline, and that was part of the package too. What they didn't know, maybe, was that he made insanely, mad passionate love to their mother every chance we got. It was wonderful, tender lovemaking such as I had never known. And he really began to love my kids and he seemed to always be there for us. He was really there for us. That first breakaway summer together was almost Arcadian.

As I mentioned before, he was a singer. Well, that's how he made a living, and things were really looking up for him. However, he had just come to Miami after a couple of years in Boston and was getting quite a number of singing jobs.

His boyish charm and appealing personality had endeared him to several of the most energetic agents in town, and before long he was clinching all the best jobs. That summer was spent together, all four of us up in the Catskill Mountains. I put my bail bonds work on hold because Jack hired me as his personal business manager, a job for which I was totally unprepared, but it gave him a reason to give me a hundred bucks a week and help me with the bills. We all traveled up to the mountains in my very jaunty Buick convertible and had a wonderful time. I had actually broken free of the mental shackles that bound me to Miami Beach and was happy to take off with this freewheeling British entertainer.

I've heard of culture shock and that sometimes people from different countries have great difficulty making certain necessary changes to accommodate a relationship with someone who had been raised with different customs and ideas. But, with my idealistic and unrealistic view of life, I thought it would be a snap. And it pretty much was.

71

Can you imagine the names I got called by my mother and other female members of the family for just packing up my kids and taking off for a summertime vacation with my handsome, adorable English lover?

Now, and for the past 20 or so years, a woman of 32, divorced and free-spirited, can do whatever the hell she likes with no one even thinking about saying anything. But back then, I was fair game. Not that I paid them any attention, mind you, told them all where to go and drove off into the sunset that I so desperately craved, but for me it was really the sunrise. And after all the crap I had been through, I felt I deserved a little happiness in my life.

I was to find out that sunrise or sunset pending, there could still be some bleak moments. It all seemed to flow so easily. A few months after the divorce Jack moved into the house because it didn't make sense for him to pay rent somewhere else when I had this big old Mediterranean Art Deco house for just me and the kids. We decided that since it was so much trouble to get a friggin' divorce, we would wait a while before we got married just to make certain that we were really in love and really compatible. My ex-husband refused to give me any child support and the court was taking forever to track the bastard down and tie up some of his loot. I was working hard, writing bonds, but still I was having a tough time. Having the large house gave me the answer and so I decided to rent out a few bedrooms. So landlady Laura I became.

The first room rental went to Jack, of course, who paid me about 20 bucks a week for the privilege of bed and board and some little added tokens of delight. Another bedroom I let off to a pair of gay friends, Freddie, a hairdresser, and his roomie Romeo, Timmy.

Both were working and paid me the great sum of $25 a week. It turned out to be a bargain for all of us. And we kept out of each other's way most of the time. It was evident that the very young Timmy had a real crush on the handsome, dashing Jack. Now on the other hand, Jack, a red-blooded straight guy who made no secret of his love for women, was bemused by the lipsticked and mustachioed pair. He spent hours, when we were all together, laughing at their unique style of dressing and their absurd makeup. But it was all in good fun and a real hoot most of the time. God, it was good to have a little laughter in my life for a change. Even my kids responded to the fun we had at the house, and in spite of the bizarre nature of some of my "roomies", we all managed to get along and have quite a good time. No pain or suffering then, and my kids were getting a very eclectic "growing up."

Freddie would style my long, golden blond hair, and design clothing I could wear to a real advantage. Then he'd take photos and make them part of his portfolio. He was a brilliant designer, and I lost quite a few sheer curtains and flowered drapes to his designing skills. He adored my bustline and created delicious bustiers, sexy blouses and other couturier concoctions with just a drape here and a few tacks there. He had a natural skill in cosmetology and always knew instinctively what would make a woman look her sexiest. Oh yes, Freddie taught me a great deal about how to apply makeup to look natural and yet exquisite.

One evening after he finished showing me how to accentuate my eyes with pale gray eye shadow he said, "Lori you have wonderfully expressive eyes, a make-up artist's dream, so blue and clear so I can create beautiful illusions and with just the right colors I can make you sexy as a siren-bitch or innocent as a doe or-"

I interrupted him, overwhelmed by all of his compliments, "stop the shit Freddie, you're making me feel very self-conscious and embarrassed."

He smiled and said "You'll see, just learn to *do* those eyes" I did. And I will always remember him.

Of course, he was in my life at a very exciting time and I shall remember him for that too. But I remember him especially when I recall an incident that was hilarious and incredibly pathetic and rang the final curtain down on my outrageous ex-husband.

The house had four bedrooms in the main part and that was what we were using. Freddie and Timmy had the master bedroom because it was the largest and sunniest and, boy, they loved the sunshine. And the moonshine. Well, Jack had the spare room, which he cleaned up. I shared a bedroom with Allison. Psychedelic posters and black light highlighted my son's room, and one never went in there if one had false teeth, because they showed up in the black light. But we were young and had all of our own teeth so there was nothing to worry about. Anyone who grew up in the '70s knows what I'm talking about.

Marshmallow, our dog, a poodle mix the color of a toasted marshmallow, slept on the bed with Allison and me and one morning about 5:30 I heard him jump off the bed and go into the dining room. A deep menacing growling sound came from within his gut, a sound I'd never heard him make before. It was eerie. Somebody was in our house, uninvited. I got chills down my spine. I could hardly speak. I knew it couldn't have been my kids. Both were spending the weekend with my mother a few blocks away, Jack was asleep, Freddie and Timmy were tucked away and their door was closed.

Then I heard Jack.

"Who the hell are you?"

There was no answer and the silence was ominous. I vibrated with the feeling that something was terribly wrong. And I was right.

What was wrong was that my blighted ex-husband, the same man who had threatened to kill me when our marriage ended, had come into the house. He didn't have to break in. I had never bothered to change the locks. And Marshmallow was the only one glad to see him. That dog never was very discriminating.

Next thing I knew my ex-husband and Jack were fighting in the dining room, both slugging it out hell bent for leather, and I ran back into my bedroom

75

and pulled out the can of Mace I had kept under my pillow for the past two years. Amazing that it still worked. But it did. Jack and the ex were all over the dining room and I just sprayed away, hoping to avoid Jack, but in a panic and moving with them, it was unavoidable. In the next few moments, Jack, who had a decided advantage in not being drunk and swaying like a dizzy cat, landed a good one on the ex's jaw and he was down for the count in an instant. But poor Jack's asthma kicked in after a good shot of Mace and he was wheezing like he'd never see tomorrow.

I heard a police siren and banging on the front door and in a flash Jack was out of there. I did not know where he went, but by the time I opened the front door for the cops, Freddie and Timmy in their sheer negligees were standing in the dining room peering down at my now unconscious ex.

Three cops barged into the house, sized up the scene and asked me, with as much seriousness as they could muster, if I had sucker-punched the poor son of a bitch lying there, bleeding like a stuck pig.

Actually, that was the first thing they asked, if I had done this to him.

I said, "No."

At that moment my ex-husband opened his eyes, looked around blearily and said, "Her boyfriend did it."

Well, the cops looked at Freddie and Timmy, and one of them said, "Which one of you is her boyfriend?"

And they burst out laughing.

I did not think any of it was funny. Poor Freddie said that he and Timmy had just been awakened by the noise of the fight and came out to see what was happening. Timmy didn't say a word.

I looked around for the now absent Jack and then told the cops that I had a restraining order, that the man on the floor was my ex-husband, as I waved the restraining order in his face.

"You bastard, you vicious bastard, that's why I divorced you. You violent son of a bitch. Get out of here, get him out of here!" I screamed.

And the cops helped him up and got him out of there.

Suddenly everything was very quiet. The ex was gone. The police told me they would file a report. I nodded in agreement. Freddie and Timmy went back to their room. Jack was nowhere to be seen. And I was alone.

Well, soon it was daybreak. I went to get a bucket and a mop to clean up the blood on the floor and suddenly I started laughing hysterically. It was the month of May and the sun came up like gangbusters and the house was filled with sunshine and my crazy laughter, and shortly, with the sound of music. Timmy was playing his guitar and, in a moment, Freddie came out with a bongo drum and I started singing, and by now we were all laughing and it was an absolutely boisterously entertaining few minutes. The tension was broken.

But, where the hell was Jack? Last I saw of him he was in his jockey shorts and was off to parts unknown - through the bathroom window, I was to find out later.

About 10 o'clock that morning Jack came banging on the back door. He had on a pair of oversized jeans and a horrible purple tie-dyed tee shirt.

"What the hell …" I began.

"Shhh," he cautioned me, "Is everything all right?"

"Some hero you turned out to be. Why, he could have killed me," I said with a straight face.

He smiled, that marvelous, charming little boy smile, filled with mischief, and said, "Not after I got done with him. By the way, who *was* that?"

"You bastard, who do you think it was? It was him, my ex."

"I don't think he'll be back," Jack said.

In fact, although a long time has passed, andI've not seen him since.

"Maybe we'll change the locks now."

So he changed the locks and everything went back to normal, at least back to what our definition of normal was at that time.

Truth be told, maybe I don't blame the poor bastard for wanting to get me. One thing I failed to mention was that one night I happened to cut the tips off all his rubbers that he stashed away while he was fucking that broad. Oh well.

Chapter Nine

In order to make a lot of money in the bail bonds business, one had to deal with a lot of our lowest class citizens; I said it before and never changed my mind. You know the kind, slick shifty-eyed wise guys who got in on the latest game in town, whatever it happened to be.

Sam was pretty careful who he let work in his office, but sometimes in the interest of making a lot of money or some good connections with powerful attorneys who in turn helped him to make lots of money, he would have someone at the office who might just be a tiny bit unsavory. Of course, it wasn't the Oval office or anything like that but a certain amount of respectability was certainly in order. Maybe. Such a person, well connected and pretty powerful as a bondsman was Harry Snow. Married 4 or 5 times, a trifle overweight and with the filthiest mouth I'd ever heard, he carried the banner in Sam's office for the most bonds. One day, as I was typing up some reports that were more than overdue, I heard Harry bellow out from his office, just down the hall from the reception area where Sherry, Sam's over-worked and over-paid secretary sat. I sat across the room from her.

"Hey, you dumb cunt, I thought I told you I needed those folders right fuckin' now".

Well, I almost died. "What did he say", I asked Sherry, kind of bewildered and in shock.

She smiled sheepishly and said to me in a low, embarrassed voice, "he wasn't talking to you- he was talking to me"

"WHAT!" I exploded, "talking to you, how dare he talk to you that way!"

So I got up and walked into Harry's office and laced into him.

"You filthy pig", I shrilled, "don't you ever, ever talk that way in this office, who the hell do you think you are?"

"I wasn't talkin' to you, sis, I was talking to Sherry, she don't mind."

Again, like a screaming skull I shrieked, "Don't call me sis! I don't care who you're talking to, don't talk like that in here, you are disgusting and I won't tolerate it."

"Sorry sis," he muttered and I stormed out of the office back to the reception area and sat down in my chair.

Sherry had her pen in hand and was on her way into Harry's office when I looked up at her and caught a tear in the corner of her eye. I just can't stand when someone attacks someone, even verbally, and for one reason or another the person is defenseless. Yeah, I'm not a fuckin goody-goody but some things are just more than I can take. Harry was pretty good natured about my attack on him - told Sam I was quite the gal.

In the early '80s, we were getting ready for the biggest drug boom ever to hit anywhere. The bond business was thriving and most of the shyster criminal lawyers, who had been plugging out a living taking thugs out of the slammer for minor crimes, were now into an almost elitist game that was fast proving itself to be quite an adventure.

With little skill, but a fierce determination, armed with writs and other legal documents, an attorney of this genre was able to convince the judge, or many judges in this fair Miami-Dade County of ours, that Pepe from Colombia was an excellent bail risk.

It was incredible. We all knew that the bastard arrived here just days before and essentially knew no one in the Miami area. Or so we thought. He was only interested in his rights from the moment of his capture.

Well, what about his inalienable rights? After all, this may be Miami, Miami Beach, or anywhere in Miami-Dade County, but it's still America with our liberal laws regarding foreigners, legal or illegal, and the lawyers who protect their rights. And speaking of rights, after the lawyer gets his call, doesn't he have the right to call upon his favorite bail bondsman?

"Who were the fine upstanding members of our community worthy of bail, and who were the worthless scumbags dredged up from a foreign shore and paid to bring horrible drugs into our fair country?" I asked Sam one fine day on our way to federal court. I shouldn't have asked.

"What are you, some fuckin' prosecutor?" he asked me, "you're making money in this business, you don't have to act like Mary fuckin' Poppins, they got a right to bail and we got a right to make the money. Any questions?"

"No", I managed to eke out.

Fortunes were begun, and fortunes were made. The White Lady, Cocaine, was making her dramatic debut in Miami Beach. And everyone wanted in on the action. Every once in a while a dirty judge or an attorney got careless and the newspapers and the FBI were on them like stink on the proverbial shit, but that took some time. And even that got cleaned up by our now most accomplished team of drug lords and lawyers.

Meanwhile, money from drug bonds was flying like the new 747s. Up, up and away. It never made any sense to me that when Carlos or Juan came in from Colombia or Peru or anywhere in South America and got busted for carrying kilos by the score and didn't have a dime on him, yet in a flash, a heartbeat, one of our top drug lawyers had him into and out of federal court. Remember Pepe from Colombia? Well, as a matter of fact, he, like, so many of the "mules," as the drug carriers came to be called, had in his pocket a slip of paper with the name of a good criminal attorney written on it. Surprise, surprise!

I couldn't give it up. Although I didn't talk to Sam about it, the questions were ever in my mind. Who put up the collateral for these million dollar bonds? And when they skipped in a few days, who was it that took the heat of paying off the courts for the bonds? Lots of questions. I'd never make a good bondsman. Immorality of the whole thing bothered me so much. So what if I'd never end up with El Rancho Grande in the best part of the city, or a million dollar condo on the Beach, or an office building on Brickell Avenue, or an association with El Banco Rico that brought me millions. I could go on and on, but, thank God that whatever drove me kept the greed quotient under control. I'm no damn saint, but the thought of being a part of what was coming, and what was here, flooding the city with drugs, was a rank experience. Who could ever know for certain what was coming next? I like to think that there is more to me than just the desire for the ultimate creature comfort at any price. But, I sort of did it for awhile longer, the bonding that is, but no drug business for me. Again, the money was pretty decent and Sammy was smart. He was very smart. He kept me away from the drug stuff. I guess he got tired of either listening to my shit or watching my face when I saw what was going on. There were still a lot of other bail bonds, other than for the druggies, waiting to be written. Smaller ones, but still it was all money coming in.

But, by the mid '80s, forget it, the Cocaine Kingpins had it all together.

Suddenly almost every one of the little criminals were taking a backseat to all of the real big money makers. No bonds written for under $25,000 were important anymore. A few years earlier the bondsmen would fight like blood thirsty tigers over a bond of a measly 10 grand, but no, not now.

The big fish were sailing the seas around Miami Beach, and they washed up on the shore with white powder in their gills. Such was the action around the bonding office that new personnel were being hired almost on a weekly basis.

Who could ever know for certain what was coming next, and how the drug scene was about to cascade into our little fortress and affect my personal life?

Chapter Ten

They say alcohol and driving don't mix. The same can be said about cocaine and guns. Something occurred that drastically changed all of our lives and made us take a realistic look at what was happening all around us, to all of us. The bubble burst.

One of Sam's best friends, and his favorite partner, was a guy named Mickey Remsen.

Mickey was a handsome, gentle and kind guy. Came from a good Jewish family that lived in Las Vegas. His parents were very old and his mother apparently had the beginnings of Alzheimers. I was very impressed that Mickey went out to Las Vegas and brought both his parents back to Miami Beach to live. One day, I mentioned this to him and he said to me very tenderly, "what else is there Lori, family, good friends, the rest is all shit. If I can make my mom and dad happy and make their lives more comfortable, well, that's it" It brought tears to my eyes, sentimental jerk that I am. Well, some things never change. And some things do. Either Mickey was handing me a line of crap, or in the next few months that man, that kind little person who so loved his parents did a complete about-face.

He and his wife, Joy, had one perfect little baby girl, and for the first time they were beginning to make some money and the future was looking rosy and bright. Sam treated Mickey well, helped him get a nice little Art Deco house on Miami Beach and gave him lots of opportunities and was a real friend to him.

Lots of gals were after Mickey and I'm not exactly sure that he said "no" all the time, but who the hell cared. He was fun at the office, never gave me any crap, and was a good bondsman. When I would write a late night bond and go to the jail with him, I felt safe and protected. He was that kind of guy. He was very respectful of me, probably because I was a little older and Sam's sister as well.

Mickey loved guns. He loved any kind of gun. He had them everywhere in his house. Mickey and Joy seemed to be getting their act together in their new home and they entertained a lot on days Mickey had off. On those few and far between days, we'd all go over for a barbecue and talk shop and invariably they would have someone staying over. Mickey had one flaw, and it would prove fatal. He drank. And he drank a lot. Guns and booze are a hot combination and are a truly deadly mix.

One Friday morning, a bright, spring, fresh-as-a-daisy day, I was driving on Alton Road on my way home from Food Fair. The radio was on playing some music when suddenly a bulletin came on. I froze as the announcer said the body of Mickey Remsen, bail bondsman, had just been discovered at his home by his wife.

"She came home to find that his head had been blown off by a single shotgun blast. The shot was apparently fired by Mr. Remsen's houseguest." The report went on to say that they had been playing Russian roulette. Both men had been drinking heavily. But I heard no more.

"Russian roulette with a shotgun, was he nuts? He must have been coked up like crazy," I said aloud. I was stunned, horrified. Leaning on my steering wheel and driving very slowly, I finally managed to get myself home. The kids were in school and the house was empty. I called my sister-in-law, Dina, Sam's wife, who was at home with Sam Jr., just a few blocks away. She said she knew what had happened and that I should come over. I did, and we both sat there and cried hysterically until we could cry no more. Poor Mickey. He was 34.

The next few days flew by in a nightmarish glare of tears and the ultimate sadness of a funeral. At that time, we thought the questions would never be answered. Why and how could this happen to one of our own? Collectively, we were a tormented lot, and Sam led the way. He never slept, and carried the responsibility of keeping everything in its proper perspective. It was a hellish time and I think the saddest part of all was that Joy was so terribly affected. Sorrow and despair ran through her like white hot shock waves and she was totally unable to cope with her loss.

I didn't see her for about three months, and then one day, while shopping, I ran into her at the market. She had lost a tremendous amount of weight and looked terribly run down. "Joy", I said, and moved closer to her "how are you? How is the baby, where have you been, are you okay?" Joy smiled a sad little smile and said, "After all that happened, I moved back to Las Vegas with Mickey's mom and dad. His mother is in a nursing home there and I am sort of taking care of his dad, I just came East to close up everything, my life is in Vegas now. Mickey's dad is really good to me and the baby and I guess I'm about as happy as I could be under the circumstances." Another sad little smile. We hugged and reminding me to send her love to Sam, she disappeared into the market. I just stood there for a long minute.

About 10 years later, we heard that she had moved to Canada and remarried. I was glad of that, but still none of us could shake what had happened. Sam, never a lover of guns, gave us all a serious lecture about a month after the shooting about the dangers of fooling around with them, as if that horrible day and the weeks that followed weren't enough of a lesson. But he had an ulterior motive in his serious discussion, and it was not for some time to come that I was able to put two and two together and come up with some answers that I never expected.

In an interesting turn of events, I found out a long, long while later, from Sam himself, over dinner at one of our favorite late-night Latin restaurants, that the day before he died, Mickey had taken out a contract on Sam. A friggin' death contract.

Mickey was willing to pay $25,000 dollars to get Sam out of the way because of some cocaine deals and other nefarious situations he had involved himself in. Knowing of Sam's aversion to drugs and dirty dealings and anything connected with them, he figured he would be dead meat himself if the truth ever got out. So he sought out someone to do the dirty on Sam, never for one minute figuring that his own days, indeed hours, were numbered.

It was a very lucky twist of fate for my brother Sammy.

What actually happened is that the day before the incident that ended Mickey's life, Sam got a telephone call from one of the bondsmen he knew in New York, who told him what Mickey was planning. But the story goes back a lot further than that. Months before, Sam had taken out of jail a high profile guy, Hymie Klosser, who had the unfortunate addiction of robbing banks. Sometimes he got away, but in at least three of the thefts he was caught, and usually with the money either on him or nearby. He was a loser of the first order, a nice guy, but a real dud. He had been able to beat some of the arrests, served two short terms because of very good lawyers, but in the final analysis the law caught up with him and wanted to put him away and throw away the key. It was only by the grace of God - and some expensive criminal attorneys - that he was even able to get a bond written for him on his latest caper.

A $50,000 bond was written by our company, and Hymie, a balding fat bastard who was still living in his mind in the heyday of his motorcycle days was out of jail, with his feet on the street. And he kept going. Within 30 days, Sam had to come up with the cash for the bond. Luckily, he was heavily collateralized. I believe that Hymie knew he was going to take it on the lam this time. The stakes were much too high for, at the very least, a 20-year prison sentence awaited him. Since he had plenty of money, why stick around? The islands of the Caribbean are havens for such as he, with lots of loot, footloose and fancy free.

Long divorced, with no kids, he'd have been nuts to stay. In the interim, before his court date and ultimate departure, and while Sam was negotiating the bond, Hymie had come up with nine diamonds. Eight of them were in small, cocktail rings, but one of them was a really spectacular unset gemstone of momentous size, three carats. Crystal clear, it was what is known as a white diamond. That means that it is D color, the best of the best, internally flawless and bringing a premium price. It was actually valued at around $50,000 at that time.

Well, Sam took it and I really believe, understanding my brother as I do, and aware of how well he knew the odds of Hymie appearing in court, that it would belong to him right at the outset. I never sat in on the meetings between Sam and Hymie, but knowing both of them, I can tell you that although Sammy is the consummate bondsman, plays it legally and always by the book, and always wants to bring the body before the court, that diamond was valuable and desirable enough to make one look the other way. Not to say that we did not do the quintessential search for this escapee. We did. And he never turned up. We searched high and low for months before the court forced us to pay up, and even then Sam kept up the march.

Sam made it clear that as soon as he paid the court for Hymie's bail bond, the big diamond was for our mother. Certainly the finest gift she would ever get. As I said, we all loved her a lot and Sam probably loved her most of all.

Sam's wife, Dina, got several of the small diamonds, but the eighth and last of the little diamond rings was a real beauty. It was antique gold with a large diamond in the center, surrounded by six smaller diamonds. It was a very pretty ring. Sam gave it to Mom who wore it every day.

Of course, years later, I got that particular ring, just before my mother died. On one of the last days of her life, she called me into her bedroom and gave me a jewelry box full of lovely rings and things. Sam had given her lots of jewelry over the years, things that had been forfeited by people who jumped bail.

She said, "Laura, I won't be here forever," because she knew that I had not yet been able to come to terms with her impending death, "and it is up to you to give the diamond rings to all of the little girl descendants that are yet to come, the grandchildren, I will never see."

I had to hold myself together while I was with her, but soon I left with the treasured little box, and I cried my heart out all that day. Still do when I think about it. She also told me to keep the little antique diamond ring and always wear it. That ring still sparkles on my finger.

And here's what happened to that lovely big unset diamond. Mickey, Sam's trusted friend, said he had a friend, a guy who was a jeweler, a diamond merchant in New York, who would set the stone in a gorgeous setting for our mother at a very reasonable price. The money was not an issue, because the guy was supposed to be the very best. Mickey took the diamond in a little pouch to New York to the jeweler he knew on 47th Street, the big Jewish diamond center in the city.

Well, when he got in the taxi, he had the diamond stashed in its little pouch in his inside jacket pocket. Lo and behold, he told us, when he got out of the cab, he discovered it was gone.

Can you imagine such a thing? Well, gone is gone. Mickey came back with the news, but no friggin' diamond, ring or otherwise. As you might well imagine, Sam got a little excited, but he had long since given up getting nuts over things. And a diamond is really just a thing. An expensive thing, but nonetheless a thing. I always wondered how Sammy was able to reconcile himself to such a loss since he had really put himself in an awkward spot to get it. But Sammy has surprised me more than once and it was soon part of the past.

Actually, I could never really forgive Mickey for what I mistakenly assumed to be his carelessness. But, in time we figured out that it was not that way at all. He never lost that diamond. The truth will never really be known, but by that time it didn't make any difference.

Mom was quite happy with her little antique diamond ring, and everything soon settled down to its usual roar around the bail bonds office.

Apparently, it took several months for Sammy to find out all that Mickey Remsen was doing apart from bail bonding. About midnight before the day Mickey died, Sam had called him and said he wanted to have a talk. Mickey, drunk and probably loaded with coke, started to cry and said to Sam, "I'm sorry, I'm no fuckin' good, I screwed it all up, that fuckin' diamond, I ruined it for everyone. Everything I touch turns to shit, I'm sorry, sorry," and hung up.

A few hours later he was dead. And that's the whole sordid story. Sam, even though he knew what Mickey had set up for him, proved himself to be a real mensch and did all the right things. Sam really liked Mickey, and it was just a horrible turn of events.

I realize now that Mickey was just an early victim of what the cocaine "business" was about to do to those who fell under its hypnotic spell, either using it, selling it, or compromising their values to get rich from it. Lots of others fared better, at least for a while.

Jack and I lived together for nearly five years and were very happy with the arrangement. Then the kids, well into their teens by now, decided it was time for us to get married. Imagine that. Seems that their friends - yep, that old peer pressure stuff - were discussing among themselves that it was strange that we had never gotten married. Guess they were all pretty straight kids and had some moral values we never even thought about.

One day Allison came home and with a sober look asked if she and I could have a chat.

Our lines of communication were always wide open, so I said, "Of course"

She said, "Mom, Chris and I had some real problems when you and Jack first hooked up. I guess we acted kind of stupid back then cause he is a nice guy but things weren't all that easy for us and we were so scared that he would want to replace our dad. But I don't know, he turned out not so bad."

So then she proceeded to say, "So why the hell aren't you guys married?"

I knew she was right and I started to wonder the same thing.

After I told Jack about my conversation with Allison earlier that day, he said.

"So, uh, what do you think about kind of getting hitched, you know, making it legal, after all it seems neither one of us is going anywhere else."

He had said, "Well, Laura," and got a very serious look on his face. He was so typically English and so goddamn cute when he was serious that it was all I could do to keep a straight face. But I did, and he continued.

"You know, a man needs a woman to be complete, and a woman needs a man to make her life right," and he smiled. He had bought me a lovely little gold ring with a smoky topaz. When he put it on my finger, I told him it would always be there. And it is.

How could I possibly have said no to such a romantic proposal? I said yes and we were off to prepare a small but very grand wedding – to be held one week later! Of course, we were on the stage a good deal of the time in those days, so we planned a late night affair, invited all the cast and our closest friends. And the following Saturday night after the performance, Jack invited everyone in the audience to our home with, "Hey folks, I'm marrying Sophia Loren tonight and you're all invited, so c'mon over."

And they did come over, dozens of them. It was a great wedding procession back to the house where our very best friends had prepared food and champagne and a huge wedding cake. Our friend and attorney, Paul Edwards, married us in front of our fireplace at midnight. What a romantic night.

My friends said we were like Snow White and Prince Charming. Jack's career was doing well and so was mine. He was appearing at a dinner theatre in Miami Beach on weekends in a show we wrote and produced. It was a lot of fun and had really started to pay off financially. Our partner was a nice Italian man who owned the restaurant and his partner was a real Mafioso type, sweet and gentle but tough as nails. Lucky for us, we soon discovered that he loved us, and since he had friends in high places in the musician's union, we were permitted to do our show with a minimum of musical accompaniment. Good thing, too, because we didn't have the money for a big orchestra.

The children had adjusted and never heard from their biological father. I had tracked the rat down and got child support for a minimal period of years while he was living with a local divorcee, but the story I got was that she caught on sooner than I did and tossed him out after a year. That may not have been the whole truth. Actually, her ex-husband had been a gangster and was murdered on the street in Miami Beach, and my poor bastard ex-husband thought he might be next so he cut and ran. He never was a hero, but who could blame him in this instance?

And then the child support stopped. Who cared? Not me, I had a handsome husband, decent work, and a nice big house on Miami Beach, which we all busted our asses to pay for.

I was coming pretty close to giving up working for Sammy. I had too much responsibility and was not making enough money to warrant all the work and time. I was doing a lot of skip tracing, locating deadbeat people who jumped bail, and I really enjoyed that aspect of the work and got better and better at it. Then a friend of mine suggested I go for my private investigator's license since I had such a natural feeling for that kind of work. What he really said was: "You're so damn nosy, you'll make the best goddamn investigator that ever walked the streets. Why the hell don't you make a living out of it?"

Made sense to me. But the time was not exactly right. I knew I would have to go back to school and take some criminal justice courses, and there was just not enough time for me to do this. So my P.I. career had to go on hold for the time being.

Since Jack knew that I had always been involved in acting, TV production and theatre one way or another in my early days, he came up with an idea that really floored me. Of course, I had done amateur theatre and played the part of Hamlet's Ophelia in a production done by a local Shakespearean theatre group. Later on I was offered a part in a Roaring 20s spectacle and loved playing the part of a jazzy siren, dancing and shimmying my way through the entire show. Currently, in our own show, I was working with Jack in every capacity - writer, stagehand, director, lighting or sound person - using my prior knowledge from working in TV. Jack told me time and again that I did a great job no matter what I did. And it was always music to my ears. But this? Whoa. We found out that the girl who had been playing the lead comedy role had developed a serious back problem and had to bow out of the show. That presented a very serious problem for us since she was one of our dancers as well. A dancer could easily be replaced, but who could play the female lead? Me, that's who.

Jack suggested that in light of my extremely well proportioned, sexy build, plus my acting skills, I might just fit the part perfectly.

The following week I was on stage. And I loved it. The lead comedienne's part was that of a real old time movie star type of character, and I was finding out that it suited me perfectly. Daytime bondsman, part time investigator, and weekends, out of the shadows came the little blonde bombshell. We booked in for the winter season at a small dinner theatre. Jack and the kids were tickled by my dedication to my newfound art. The audiences seemed pleased enough. I got to shimmy and sparkle a bit but of course, Jack was the star, no question about that.

To this day, I am still reluctant to give too many details of this caper for fear of recriminations, but the story must be told. They say one picture is worth a thousand words. Sometimes a picture can be worth a quarter of a million dollars, given the right picture of course. And if, as is in this case, all the local, state and federal photos of an escaped criminal mysteriously disappeared from the files, well, what would that picture be worth?

Chapter Eleven

One day Jack got a call from his favorite agent, a charming and debonair man in his '80s. He had been very active in show business in the early '20s on Broadway, the vaudeville circuit and Tin Pan Alley. He reminded me of George Burns, even down to the cigar. A few years earlier, he had retired to Miami to live out his last golden days in semi-retirement, but the pull of show business tugged at his heart, and got him back onto his feet and into a theatrical office where he spent his days booking a lot of the shows around town. His nights were devoted to checking out his acts in all the many theatres and night clubs around Miami Beach.

I loved old CJ because he shared my passion for the hot sweet poison called Café Cubano, and many nights while Jack, my true love, was out singing at a club or a theatre, CJ and I would sneak out and get a colada. He loved doing that as much as I did.

"Listen, Jack," he said one afternoon on the telephone, "I got a real deal for ya pal, ya open at the Gigi Room at the Fontainebleau next Monday. The money ain't bad, five hundred smackeroos. Take you out of that little dive you play on weekends, put some class in your act."

Well, I soon got over my chagrin at the insult about our little showplace, and we were over the moon with joy about Jack's playing the Gigi Room. It was the hottest cabaret in town and all the great acts played there. So the entire family, my brothers and their wives and many of our friends, made plans to be there for the big opening night.

What an opening night it turned out to be. In Miami Beach in those days, before condos destroyed the view of the ocean and it was still safe to go out at night to a show, there were lots of hotels showcasing the biggest stars of all time.

At that time you could see Tom Jones, Englebert Humperdinck, Liza Minelli, Frank Sinatra and dozens of others appearing at all the big hotels and Sunrise Musical Theatre. Great shows, good dinners, fine wines, all available at reasonable prices. There I go again, sounding like a commercial. A retro-commercial, to be sure. But Jack was a truly unique performer. The sound and quality of his voice were reminiscent of the famous singer Al Jolson, whose professional career went from the turn of the 20th century, into talking movies and from there to a brilliant Broadway career. He was known worldwide and many tried to imitate him after his death. Jack sounded just like him. We were making the most of it.

Then another twist of fate came sashaying into our private and public lives, this time really involving all of us, but primarily brother Sam. It was a most extraordinary time for Sammy. He had just gotten a guy out of Federal prison on a $250,000 bond. A little, and I mean little, foreign gentleman, a dapper sort of guy whose demeanor in no way reflected his criminal behavior. Little did we know.

Cecil La Tour was his name, and he was charged with drug trafficking and the usual conspiracy charges. We had taken a lot of collateral from the guy who, it turned out, was known as the Robin Hood of the Bahamas, the chain of tropical islands directly east and south of Miami Beach. It was the first bond that Sam had ever written for a quarter of a million dollars and we were all very excited, and in my case a bit apprehensive about it.

The way the bonding situation works is that if and when a person skips, or fails to appear for his or her first trial appearance, the bondsman has a certain amount of time to produce the person. "Bring the body before the court" is the way it reads. Then, after that time elapses, the bond is forfeited and the bondsman has to produce the person or the money within a certain time. Cold cash is required to satisfy the court. And there are a number of ways it can be obtained. Most often, the bondsman will call in the

101

bond and ask for cash from the family or the person who actually guaranteed the bond.

Failing that, the bondsman has the right to sell off any personal or real property that he is holding as collateral. In this particular case, we had lots and lots of collateral. Unfortunately for us, it was all held in the Bahamas, close in miles to Florida, but a foreign country. And so the fun began. Yeah, little Cecil owned plenty of items that he assured us could be turned into ready cash. Things like sailboats and airplanes and beachfront houses. So we were prepared to sell. Right.

It seems little Cecil La Tour trafficked in cocaine and spent his money like water to house, feed and clothe, his enormous far-flung family and many other Bahamians as well. He was loved and sorely missed now that he was in jail in Miami awaiting his trial with a federal prison sentence almost a certainty. We were soon to find out just how loved he was. Cecil stayed at Sam's and Dina's house. It was not exactly Cecil's choice of places to reside while out on bond, but Sam felt it necessary to keep a constant eye on him and the only way he could do it was to keep him in his own home.

So, they worked it all out and Sam gave Cecil a place to stay at his house, a nice little room just off the living room downstairs. The door was locked with a key at night and the windows sealed shut. And so in that way Cecil would remain close to Sam until the trial, about two months away. A quarter of a million bucks is a lot of dough.

He was a simple, unassuming, almost humble little guy who smiled a lot and was very friendly. He was also shackled to Sam with leg irons whenever they left the house.

Well, the big night was fast approaching and Sam did not want to take a chance on missing out on the GiGi opening. So he shackled Cecil up by connecting his footcuffs to himself, and the two guys, more attached than usual, went out to the driveway and got into the back of Sam's Caddy, and Dina drove them to the Fontainebleau Hotel. That might sound a little bizarre, but the cuffs of their pants pretty much covered the chain, and anyway who was looking?

It was a glamorous night, the kind you dream of when you're in show business and we all wore long dresses and were dressed up like Lady Astor's pet horses. The aura of an opening night filled the air as we all settled in for a good show. Backstage, Jack was flying around like a nervous wreck, so I decided the best place for me was out front with the family.

The orchestra was playing dance music, and for me it was truly the beginning of an incredibly special evening. After an extraordinary dinner and before Jack came out, the house photographer asked if we'd like pictures. Sam, the sport that he is, and knowing what a festive occasion this was, told her to go ahead, and make sure to get everyone in. She did and the pictures were marvelous, but, somehow in the great explosion of excitement that followed Jack's performance, we did not buy any of the photos. It was purely an oversight, and the photographer was really busy selling like crazy to all the other tables. Those pictures were eventually to play a very important part in this story.

It was one of the most wonderful nights of Jack's career up to that point. The audience was overwhelmed by his talent and stage presence, and there were bows after bows and at least a half-dozen curtain calls. The orchestra was in perfect sync with him and I had never seen a more perfect show. The night ended amidst lots of congratulations and thanks for a wonderful evening.

As Sam and Cecil, still shackled together, limped out to the valet to get the car, we all had a good laugh. It really was quite hysterical. At the time Sam was pretty heavy and heads taller than Cecil and yet here he was chained to this 5' 2" black man as they zigged and zagged their way into the car. They had to get into the back seat together again, this time in full view of a roaring crowd of friends and family, and it was hilarious to see.

Little did we know our laughter was to be short lived.

That's how it is in this business of crime, you just never know what could be around the corner. Sometimes you trip and fall and break a toe or a leg and get laid up for months, no money coming in. Other times you can trip and fall and end up with a huge windfall, because it turned out to be someone else's carelessness that caused the fall. Just the luck of the draw.

Sam was a master at what he did. His decisions were usually very sound and spot on and his lucrative bail bonds business was certainly on the way up. He knew how to cover his ass, protect his assets and build success and security into all his adventures. His generosity was well known and soon he would be famous or infamous depending on who was looking from coast to coast.

But a dark adventure was looming that threatened his business and possibly even his life and the lives of those near and dear who worked for him. A great dilemma was soon presented that tested his integrity and placed him on the threshold of disaster.

Chapter Twelve

After his Fontainebleau success and the close of our dinner theatre run, lots of work came in for Jack and we met a multimillionaire who set up a Tony Awards show spot for him at Broadway's premier theatre. For a gal who had been used to Miami and its little night life scene of the '60s and '70s, New York was indeed the Big Apple, with a capital A. What a place, sin city! Even Jack, my Mr. Clean, came alive while we were there and got caught up in the spicy, sexy feel of little old New York. We had some hot times in the old town. And I could hardly wait to get back there.

Meanwhile, my bail bond work and my investigative career were beginning to effectively come together, and I was doing some interesting preliminary detective work for a few of the attorneys I knew. Mostly it was still locating people. Not very different from my skip tracing stuff. There was perhaps just a shade of difference inasmuch as I was asking for more money for my services and spreading out a bit into the legal field. Most important to me was that I was beginning to feel like an investigator. And I began to sort out a plan in my head about going back to school to take the courses that would qualify me for a P.I. license. Sam wrote lots of bonds and I still helped on some of them, but after the excitement of New York, I was feeling kind of bored.

Eventually, Cecil LaTour had his day in court and Sam unshackled the little bastard so the judge would not have a stroke in the courtroom. Turns out that it would have been better for the judge to have the stroke then and there instead of what happened later, over the next few months.

As the bailiff and the court reporters were settling in on the third day of his trial, Cecil told Sam he was going to the bathroom. Sam, tied up in his own pre-court-day procedures, agreed and in a flash Cecil was up and out, like a rat out of a trap. Sam looked around as the court was about to come to order. Cecil was not there. He was gone. And yes, there was no Cecil for a long, long, expensive time to come.

We rushed down to Sam's car, his wonderful electric blue Cadillac - the bail bondsman's ultimate dream car - and it was nowhere in sight. Our little Cecil and Sam's car had run off together. They found it two days later at the airport. The Cadillac, not Cecil. The skinny little ingrate left a note of thanks for Sam. At least he was grateful for his freedom. How the hell he managed to get out of

Miami and fly to the Bahamas without a passport is still a mystery to all of us.

Jack and I played a part in this little sad but exciting tale because for some reason unbeknownst to Sam or anyone at federal court, there were no pictures available of Mr. Cecil LaTour. Except for one. Remember the night at the Fontainebleau? Well, so did we. We rushed over and found the lady photographer who, for $100, sold us the negative. And there was dear old Cecil, shackled invisibly under the table, smiling away at the camera.

After a quick and very lucrative deal was made, especially for the photographer, we got the negatives and had them made up into prints immediately. The regular posters- and others, written in Spanish and called *"buscando* or wanted- were made by the thousands. His bond was for a mere quarter of a million bucks but it is expensive to look for someone like Cecil. Cecil could go back to his native Bahamas and have a million places to hide out. And he did. And Sam looked. And paid. And followed every lead. The world swallowed up little Cecil and closed around him.

Then Sam had to arrange to pay the forfeited bond. The federal court asked for a quarter of a million bananas. That's $250,000. Sam, being the sharpshooter that he is, had taken that much in collateral from Cecil when he initially wrote the bond.

Thus began my personal involvement in this saga, and it is only by the grace of God that I am here to tell it. It all sounded so great. Get on a plane, fly down to the Bahamas - actually to Nassau, the capital - just a quick 30-minute trip down to the land of tropical breezes, sunshine and white sand beaches. It was the picture-postcard dreamland of every cold and winter-weary inhabitant of the dear old U.S. of A. Even though I live in Miami, that particular paradise is just around the corner. And it's nice to get away, so when Sam sweetened the pot with a hundred bucks a day, I thought I'd be a fool to turn it down. Maybe. Boy, was I wrong.

Without my even knowing it, the very first time I set foot on that plane to go to Nassau, my investigative career went into high gear. And a hundred bucks a day back then, plus expenses, wasn't too bad, especially for a novice.

Arriving in Nassau was always fun, hearing the tropical sounds of calypso music skillfully played by Bahamian steel bands at the airport. Swaying, tall coconut-laden palm trees lined the sides of the road to town. I took a taxi. It was a real bargain, about 10 bucks all the way into town. The Bahamians were still under English rule at that time and the city of Nassau was very British indeed. The cars drove on the left. In the center of town near the British Colonial Hotel, a fine old pink structure reflecting the best days of the British Empire and its gifts to the colonies, was a little island whereupon stood, in full British regalia, a traffic warden. In his white suit, with navy blue banner, red decorations and white pith helmet, he was indeed a sight for the tourists to behold. And he worked hard. No easy job to direct a bunch of American tourists accustomed to driving on the right and having to stay on the left. Of course, with few exceptions, no American had ever even seen a roundabout, much less had ever driven on one. But our man in his starched white uniform was more than equal to the task and there was never any problem that I could see. His efficiency and competency were a credit to his fine British training.

My taxi pulled up at the bottom of Parliament Hill and in a short time I was up the hill and inside the Government House. I was amazed at how similar the surroundings were to what I had seen in movies of courthouses in England. Except that here in the tropics the building was almost open air with a lovely lattice breezeway where the graceful tropical breezes swept through and kept the structure cool and airy. I chose to take the circular staircase to the second floor. Then I was in a large spherical room with three little cage-type windows and a clerk behind each one.

Their earnest, sincere smiling faces assured me that these were very capable and qualified personnel and I would most certainly be in good hands. As I opened my briefcase and took out the legal papers that I carried, the clerk looked at me and said,

"Do you know what these papers are?"

"Of course," I replied. "I am foreclosing on properties owned by Cecil LaTour to compensate for the forfeiture of his bond in the federal court in Miami because of his drug trafficking."

Had I stuck a knife in her belly I would not have seen a more pained expression.

"Anything wrong?" I queried.

"Nnnno," she stammered and asked me to wait for just a moment.

The cage clunked shut and I was standing there alone. All the sound in the room had ceased and the silence shattered my tenuous equilibrium. It seemed like my center of gravity was in my chest cavity and my heart was beating like one of the steel drums I had heard just a little bit earlier at the airport. Something was wrong. And I did not know what, or what to do about it.

About three minutes that felt like three hours passed and the clerk appeared once again and asked me if I had notarized the documents.

"Yes, I prepared the documents while I was still in Miami," I replied.

"Sorry," she said, "You will have to do them here in front of me."

"Why, that's impossible," I said, my voice barely audible. "I do not have my notary seal with me. I left it back in my office in Florida," I stammered in a staccato voice.

"Then we cannot process these documents," she informed me, in no uncertain terms.

"But," I managed to squeak out, and then the cage shut again and I knew I was out of luck. I tried to get her attention once again, but it was to no avail. And the other two cages had closed down as well. There was nothing left for me to do but take my papers and stuff them back into the briefcase and backtrack down the stairs, through the breezy hallway and out to the street. I shuffled down Parliament Hill and gathered myself together.

I thought to myself, it's still early, so I'll go over to Blackbeard's Tavern, have some lunch, maybe a rum punch to steady my nerves, and then go to the Paris shop for some perfume I'd promised my mother. So I did.

The return trip was uneventful and I arrived at the office about 4 o'clock as Sam was meeting with Paul Edwards, one of the criminal attorneys involved in the Cecil LaTour case. When they saw me they were a happy pair, certain that the foreclosure proceedings on Cecil's valuable land, boats, and airplanes had been accomplished. The thought of being off the hook for a quarter of a million dollars brought delighted smiles to their faces. It was short lived when my little bombshell exploded.

"What?" a perplexed Sam exclaimed after I told them the sad little tale.

Paul threw up his hands in disgust and said, "I was afraid this would happen. The little bastard is their idol, and they ain't gonna help us one iota."

"What can we do?" Sam asked Paul, and his reply was that we could just keep going down there and try to wear them down. He said it was really just a temporary setback and they had no legal right to keep us from foreclosing on Cecil's property. Right.

The following Wednesday, very early in the morning, armed with my notary seal and stamp, I once again boarded an Eastern Airlines plane from

Miami International Airport bound for the beautiful Bahamas. Somehow the music sounded a little tinny this time. The sun was shining and it looked like this unfortunate turn of events would soon be resolved and I would be back at my favorite perfume shop in no time at all.

The taxi trip was fast, faster than I remembered, and the climb up the hill was even quicker. Once again the three little cages had smiling faces behind them, and as I approached the center cage, the smile faded, but the innate, thoroughly starchy, British politeness was clearly evident.

"How can we help you?" the woman inquired of me.

"Well, I'm here about the Cecil LaTour foreclosure and I'm prepared to notarize these papers in front of you," I said, as I took the papers from the briefcase and put them on the counter.

The woman looked at me with the coldest stare I had ever seen and said, "I'm sorry but the person who looks after that is not here today. She is terribly ill and won't be back for some time."

What a nice English accent she had.

What could I say? I was feeling lots of things, none of them productive. I wanted to tell the stupid bitch that I had traveled all the way from Miami to get these goddamn papers filed and I was really pissed off. Somehow I knew she was aware of that.

Smiling, I said, "Oh, I am so sorry, perhaps I can come back here at another time."

She gave me a knowing, unsmiling look and crossed her arms over her chest as she replied "Yes, you do that."

I turned and left the office and hurried down the steps. Somehow, the warmth of the morning had turned to a chill and I couldn't wait to get out of there. Safe again on the street, I did my shopping and stopped for a quick lunch at Blackbeard's Tavern- shepherd's pie and a glass of ale. Blackbeard's Tavern just about the only place one can get such marvelous English food outside of London. The day brightened up again for me and so I strolled along the lovely bayfront and after an hour or so took a taxi back to the airport.

Back at the office, Sam took the news pretty well, considering. He told me we would let some time pass, maybe two weeks or so, and then he would have me return. He said he would pay me another hundred bucks, sport that he was. Anyway, that was two day's pay I had earned while having some fun in the sun. Life isn't all bad.

But it can get a lot worse, as I soon found out. The fun in the sun turned to terror in the tropics.

Chapter Thirteen

About a month after my last trip to the Caribbean, Sammy decided that enough time had passed and it would be feasible for me to go back down to the islands on the Cecil LaTour situation. He was still at large and costing Sammy a lot in actual cash laid out for search expenses, and more importantly, real worries about the business going under if he had to pull a quarter million bucks out of the air and plunk it down in front of the judge.

"Time is getting short," he told me.

So I packed up the old briefcase and boarded Eastern Airlines flight 100 at 8 a.m. on a sunny Tuesday. With luck I'd be back for the matinee on Thursday. We liked to have a short rehearsal on Wednesday afternoons, to shake up the gang after a few days off, so Tuesday was the most appropriate time for me to go.

When I landed in the Bahamas it was raining and the taxi ride was a slip and slide affair all over the muddy road. Up the hill I went to see my surly friends in their cages. Perhaps it would be different this time. Oh yes, it was different this time. The moment I walked into the office from the breezeway, and the clerks saw me, all three cages closed down.

That's right. Shut. I must admit I was bewildered, but not so naive that I did not know what was going on.

"Out," I said to myself. "And fast." Down the windswept corridor, down the steps and out to the lawn in front, actually it was top of Parliament Hill. Then, to my total surprise, I saw that a new item had been added to the rainy and foreboding landscape. At the curb and shining like an enormous polished jet jewel sat a long black shiny Cadillac limousine with darkly tinted windows.

God help us all, was my first thought. Followed by *get down the hill*, quickly. And then, *what the fuck is going on here*? So, down the hill I went.

In Nassau at that time, there were no public telephone booths. All calls had to be made from the telecom center at the bottom of the hill. I was glad that I had spent some time wandering around on my previous visits, so I knew about the telecom center. As I entered the small building, I looked back over my shoulder and saw the limousine slowly coming down the hill. Speaking to the receptionist at the front gave me back my voice, and I told her I wanted to place a call to Miami.

"Take the booth on the right, number four," she said, as she took my 10 dollars.

It was very expensive to call the States in those days. I went into the semi-dark telephone booth. It was hot and muggy in the telecom center, no bright lights and no air conditioning. A hard, straight upright chair, very similar to the ones used in schools, stood in the corner of the dimly lit space and above it was a telephone hand set. No dials, just a hand set. I sat down and lifted the receiver to my ear. I could hear lots of buzzing and in a moment Sam's voice came on the line.

I had given the receptionist Sam's private unlisted number. Somehow I knew I should not place a call to the office switchboard. When Sam answered, I told him what had happened.

He said, "Hold on, I want to connect us with someone." In a moment, Paul was on the line. I spoke very little as Sam filled him in adding a kind of cryptic pitch to his usual pleasant sound.

At last Paul spoke, "Listen closely, Laura," he said in a very low voice. "Get off the island NOW, do not pass go, do not collect two hundred dollars. Do not go shopping, come home now."

I started to shake. Although Laura was my given name, everyone always called me Lori and calling me Laura meant someone really wanted to get my attention because of some unusual happening or was really pissed off at me. I knew immediately this was a serious issue.

Paul went on, his voice growing more and more husky.

"Listen to me, the only reason you are still okay, maybe even still alive," he paused, "is that they don't know who you are."

He went on, "Do you understand me?"

He was speaking very fast, so fast that his words were practically unintelligible to me, and, I realized, to anyone who might be listening to the conversation.

Then I really began to shake.

"Now, hang up and do what I told you you must," he said in a most commanding voice.

I said I would. No muddling here, I understood every word.

Walking out the door and onto the street and having the rain hit me in the face, brought me back to myself and to the reality of just what was happening. Waiting at the curb in front of the telecom center was the big, black Cadillac limousine. In front of the limousine was a taxi. The taxi pulled up and the driver opened the door. I knew I had no choice so I got in.

The limousine followed us on the slow drive to the airport. At least I hoped and prayed we were going to the airport. I was terrified and the driver did not speak even one word to me. By now I knew the route pretty well, so as we rounded the last bend to approach Nassau International Airport, I said thank you to God and closed my eyes. The taxi driver pulled up in front and opened my door, I had a 10 dollar bill in my hand, which I rather tentatively moved toward the driver, but he unsmilingly waved it away.

To this day, I cannot remember walking into the terminal. That part of my adventure seemed to fade away. Not a word was spoken until, once inside the terminal, I handed my ticket to the agent.

"Can I get on the next flight to Miami?"

Obviously the agent did not know who I was, so she smiled and said, "Sure."

Was I ever in a paranoid condition. The next flight was in 30 minutes and it was the longest 30 minutes I had ever spent.

Back again on the ground in Miami, I started to feel a little bit better, still scared, though.

"Was I followed?" I allowed myself to whisper out loud, and then there at the curb, waiting in the misty midmorning half gloom, were Sam and Paul Edwards. I didn't collapse until I got into the car. As we drove back to the office, Sam explained the reason for their serious concern. As if being followed around by a big, black limousine on the island wasn't enough.

"If they knew who you were, if they knew you were my sister, you would have been kidnapped and held until I stopped trying to find and bring back Cecil," he told me, and Paul nodded in agreement.

Sam said, "That was a close call, and we won't do it again."

"Well, thank you very much," I sarcastically spewed out. "Maybe I can just stay here in Miami Beach and live my life."

119

In the next few months lots of feedback came in response to our sending out posters all over the United States and the Caribbean looking for the missing Cecil LaTour. It seemed to us that he had been swallowed up, and because none of the reported sightings were viable, he seemed to have disappeared off the face of the earth.

Cecil didn't turn up for about a year. After many false leads, heartbreak for Sam who had to fork over the quarter of a million bucks, and a good deal of frustration at the office, we finally got a workable lead. Cecil was spotted in a large tropical island in the Caribbean. It was Jamaica. Having been seen several times, by different people. It looked like little Cecil was getting careless.

Sam and my youngest brother, Brad, decided to hire what we refer to in the trade, as bounty hunters. Trusted, strong and silent, this was Sam's omnipotent army. Bail bondsmen have incredible power in the United States, within federal and state laws, to apprehend felons who have escaped. Not so out of the country, particularly in Third World areas. And the island nations certainly fall into this category.

Armed with writs and all sorts of legal documentation as to the right of Sam and company to bring this individual, known as Cecil LaTour, back to the jurisdiction of the United States, they set off via a local airline that flew once a day to Jamaica.

This airline flew to most of the Caribbean islands and was very popular with American tourists seeking a bit of fun and sun in the tropics.

Eventually, Brad told me that on the flight out, he, Sam and Hugo, Sam's favorite bounty hunter, carefully planned just how this operation would take place.

Hugo was black, originally from Mexico. Spanish and Indian blood coursed through his very large ropy veins and he spoke softly in Spanish, moreover he thought in Spanish and at times expressed himself with a lot of expletives. Hugo was a giant of a man, all 6' 6" of him. He was always very gentle and smiled whenever he saw me, but I could see the power in his mighty arms and legs and feel the blood that worked behind his eyes. Fiercely protective of Sammy, he was never more than a heartbeat away from his side. And it was easy to see why Sammy had decided to take him along on this mission. They had pretty good information as to where Cecil was hiding, and a detailed map of the island showing just where he would be in relation to the airport and the hotel where they would stay. Of course all this data was relative to his LKA, his last known address.

Things can change very quickly for a man on the run. And Cecil was on the run.

This island of Jamaica was not his home territory, and although the native Jamaicans were friendly, it was not like being on home base. Actually, it must have cost him a fortune to finance the escape and hide out for such a long period. Apparently that was no problem for Cecil. He had a fortune. We had recently received good information that Cecil was not alone in his escape plan. He had lots of help, unbeknownst to us, of course. We knew he had good connections in the states, and drugsters help each other out when necessary. Truly, it was just like a family, a family of great fellows that conspire to make drugs available to our kids. Such a folksy thing to do.

It seems that there was a link in the Miami Beach courthouse to one of the drug families. A "nice girl" who needed a few extra bucks or drugs now and then, and knew how to keep her mouth shut when necessary. She spied for the defendant and gave secret prosecution details to the defense. For her efforts she was well rewarded, got a bit of coke, some money and 15 years in the slammer for aiding and abetting. Nice while it lasted, though.

I interviewed her prior to a bond hearing and it was clear she was full of shit about being a victim. Her dishonesty and guilt waved like a red flag in our faces and because of her, a desperate criminal, albeit a seemingly nice guy, was out of our jurisdiction and on the lam. Bond was denied and there was talk of the possibility of a charge of treason coming out of the conspiracy charge, a federal charge levied against most drug traffickers. She was an American citizen, born and raised in Miami. May God bless America.

Brad, my youngest brother, was a real cowboy at that time. Motorcycles and hot, sexy blondes were soon to be replaced by a loving swami and vegetarian dinners, but then it was non-stop excitement and the go-go girls in his life never seemed to come to a stop-stop.

He said it was sort of like a ring of fire that he went through and he couldn't stop until its time had passed. I reflect on that sometimes and wonder if lots of us don't go through that very same consciousness and yet are not in touch with ourselves enough to pin a tag on it like Brad did. Truly it seemed to be a rite of passage. Eventually he changed his modus operandi and became quite a conservative fellow indeed.

The end was nigh, but not nigh enough. Cecil, discovering that his archenemies and would-be captors were in town, did a real good job of disappearing.

English, of sorts, is spoken in Jamaica where Sam and his money found many willing hands to reach out for this would-be Robin Hood of the Bahamas. Back at the ranch, we just had to wait and hope. Since this all happened in the early '80s and cell phones were not in widespread use, it was hard to transmit information from the island to us. That was mostly because the bounty hunters could not take the risk of being overheard, and the little black cat slipping out of the bag.

On the second day of their mysterious journey, Sam called and told me to hop on the next plane to Jamaica. It seems he felt that I would be a great asset in helping to track down little Cecil.

"A little female color never hurts, Lori, especially when she looks like you." he explained.

And then he went on, "They never see blue-eyed blondes down here, not built like you, except if they're staying in the hotels, and then they're unapproachable."

I interrupted with, "So what am I supposed to be, little brother, approachable? If you think that I am going to bring my sweet ass down there to be used as a shill, or something even worse, well, you can just . . ."

Laughing, he interrupted me this time. "No, no, nothing like that, dear Sister. You'll just provide, shall we say, a bit of diversion. And, of course, you'll be on pay."

The magic words did the trick. *Might be fun down there,* I ventured to myself *and I'd certainly be protected.* Why, Hugo himself could virtually stop an armored truck. So, what the hell.

"Okay, you got a deal, have Sherry send me a ticket."

"No time for that," was his immediate reply. "Go to the office, have Sher make a reservation, and pay for it immediately. There's a six o'clock flight to Kingston. We'll pick you up at the airport."

Sam hung up.

I did as he asked. His wonderful and loyal secretary, Sherry, was overworked and overpaid, as I've said before, and well worth it for she was more than a secretary - she was his right arm. Sherry made the reservation and paid for the trip. At 8:30 that evening I cruised gently on silver wings into Kingston International Airport in the bustling and bawdy Caribbean country of Jamaica. Right into the arms, more or less, of my two tired but incredibly optimistic brothers.

Chapter Fourteen

The hotel had seen better days. Seedy and downbeat was a kindly understatement. But the rooms were clean and cheery and luckily Sam had arranged for me to have my own. It was up near the top of the small building, and filled with lots of redolent, exotic colorful flowers. Caribbean varieties of sweet-scented frangipani, white with brilliant orange centers, and a yellow ginger plant, filled the air with the fragrance of expensive champagne. In the center of the small room, on a mahogany table, was a large pot filled with the mysterious flower Plumbago, brilliant with its distinct aromatic flavor and glittery purple color.

Noise was the issue of the day, an unbelievable cacophony of various sounds filling the air with its loudness as the sounds of children, clamorous

Caribbean music and laughter came wafting up from the sidewalks below.

I settled in and was glad for a rest after an eventful day of preparing and finally traveling to this beautiful, far away, yet strangely familiar island paradise. I didn't know enough to reserve judgment on the word paradise.

It was pleasant spending the first few days with my brothers and Hugo. Heaven knows we were all too busy in Miami to have much quality time together. So, maybe it was paradise. And maybe it wasn't.

We had most of our meals in the small cafe in the hotel. No matter how limited the accommodations, there was always some sort of food establishment, and the food was good, native and hot, chicken and fish prepared with finesse and great care. The superb blending of island spices and real know-how combined to make our meals Epicurean delights. This pleased us no end, for our entire family takes great pleasure in the preparing and sharing of food. On the next night, our landlady surprised us with a curried goat. God, although it smelled all right, it was a bit gamey, but covered with enough spice to make an ordinary person forget or not take heed of exactly what it was. Momentarily I considered fasting instead of feasting, but there were some lovely green, succulent looking vegetables on the sideboard along with some Malanga, sweet potato puffs, and a good slice of mango for desert. I was in gastronomical heaven.

About the third day I was a guest on the busy little island of Jamaica. Some local decided big bucks were a little more awe-inspiring than loyalty to a stranger who had come into their midst and created a lot of chaos among them all. Let me tell you, at that point, it seemed that havoc became the middle name of the big, bad brothers from Miami.

"Meet us down by the south docks," was all that a tired and sleepy Sammy heard in a cryptic phone call that came at a little past 5 in the morning. The call was no surprise, but it brought some shock waves with it just the same. Weeks later, Hugo confessed to me that just before the inevitable moment of truth, or capture, he got scared shitless, all 6' 6"of him.

We went to the docks and no one was there. At least we saw no one. I flashed my pretty blonde self along with Sammy as Brad and Hugo waited in the car. Actually, we were all bondsmen, give or take a technicality here and there as to gender.

The bail bondsman, as I have said before, has unbelievable and incredible rights in the United States. All over the United States. A federal statute called Taylor v. Taintor, passed around 1868 and never revoked, gave bondsmen the right to break down doors to enter a property where an escaped felon was believed to be hiding, to arrest on the Sabbath, and to have the right to house their prisoner in any remote jail anywhere in the country. Also the right to use a weapon if force was necessary. Pretty tough stuff.

Well, that's in the States. In Jamaica, as in most foreign countries, all that was unknown. If you got caught with a gun, it was big trouble. You could really be in the shit. But there were certain extenuating factors that kept you from getting caught with the gun. Paying off the local constabulary was the primary safety factor. Killing the bastard and dumping him at sea was another. And there was enough sea. Neither of these solutions could be applied in this situation, so the great brains had to think up another way to resolve their problem. As to their popularity, bail bondsmen and bounty hunters were certainly not particularly well received in those places and had no standing with the law, or even with the populace in general, except in certain cases where a good deal of cash swept across their palms. Not that that's so strange, considering what goes on here in Miami, Florida where the old cliché "land of the outstretched palm" is right at home.

So what?

We had been there about half an hour and were all sweaty. Where were the balmy breezes of Caribbean advertising fame? Suddenly three guys appeared out of nowhere and told Sam they had Cecil holed up in an old hotel on the other side of the island. They said for 10,000 American dollars they would turn him over. Bingo! It seemed to be as simple as that.

Hugo wanted to bang their heads together, but they all knew that would serve no purpose and at that point the 10 G's were incidental. Could we trust the little bastards? Probably not, but what was the alternative? Too much invested to turn back now. Brad carried the money and counted out the 10 grand in hundreds and gave it to one of the men. He was a slimy little snake if ever there was one.

About an hour later, a long hour of sitting at the dock and just waiting, a car pulled up with two people in it, a black guy, small, skinny and toothless, and the driver, another little Jamaican who promptly told Sam and Hugo to get in.

Brad and I, "La Señorita," were to wait.

"No way, we're a team, a fuckin' team," Brad screamed out, and pushing me ahead of him, we both got in the car with the others.

Brad was a hothead. My mother worried he would wear out all of his parts before he was 30. He is surely living proof that doesn't happen. Fearless and dauntless, he paved the way for some of the bounty hunters that crossed our paths. Even Hugo, the toughest guy I'd ever met, told me that Brad was totally out of whack concerning the apprehension of a criminal on the run. Regardless, they all followed his lead and somehow Brad survived the recklessness of his youth and came out the other side a better person.

It was a long ride in an old junker with me in the back squeezed in between Brad and Hugo, and Sammy in the front with the driver and the other skinny little guy. In about an hour we were there. A hot, stinking, crowded hour. Like a flash, as soon as we parked, they were up the stairs of ths old, broken-down hotel in the middle of a jungle, and seconds later they were carrying out a yelling, hooting and hollering little Cecil, whose hands and feet were tied with a rope.

I waited in the car with the two native Jamaicans, who looked like the tropical sun had warmed their gonads to the point that if Hugo had not come down in that instant, I might have been in for some Jamaican judo. Lord, help us all.

The sense of humor that Cecil exhibited to us on many occasions while in Miami was missing and he cursed and hollered during the whole ride to the airport. Then the fun began.

Sammy had called ahead and was able to secure five reservations, one each for himself, Brad, Hugo, me, and, of course, our most unwilling hostage. We were on the next flight to Miami, which was in less than an hour from the time we left the hotel.

Plenty of time to make it, the guy driving assured Sam. It was crowded and hot as hell in the car, now with seven people jammed in like sardines in a hot tin can.

"Disgusting, to say the least," Hugo told me when it was all over. And there was no choice, no turning back, no going to our hotel to get our clothes. We knew our only chance to get Cecil off the island was now, quickly, and without too much fuss. But it did not work out quite that way.

When we got to the airport, Cecil was screaming his head off. This made a very big impression on the reservation clerks and the passengers who were preparing to board the little jet out on the runway.

This airport was not exactly an international situation - three airplanes on two runways - and that was it. A control tower the size of a giant water tower stood imposingly over the small tarmac landing strips. In the next few minutes, several important things happened. First of all, the reservation clerks, terribly upset by the screaming Cecil, informed Sam that the flight would be delayed. Then a dozen passengers came up to Cecil, surrounding the entire little group of our guerilla force, and, speaking broken English, asked what was going on. Cecil screamed that he was being kidnapped and the whole scene turned into bedlam. Luckily, one of the airport administrators, more concerned for the welfare of his little kingdom than the effects of the crowd on the four Americans and one little Bahamian, ushered us all through a narrow passageway, far from the now maddened crowd.

For at least a few minutes, peace was restored as Sammy finally stuffed a man's handkerchief into Cecil's mouth, so that our nerves could get some relief and we could think of an alternate plan. Sitting on hard wooden benches in the stifling heat of a tropical Jamaican morning, Sam decided the best move would be to hire a Learjet from Miami and get Cecil home with a little privacy and a lot of quiet.

The scene that had just transpired must not be allowed to happen again. So, as Brad and Hugo went to look around the airport and think about exactly how they would transport the now bound up Cecil, Sam called Frank Timmons, a pilot friend who worked out of Fort Lauderdale. Frank, a cowboy

131

pilot who had access to almost any airplane you could ask for, provided you could pay for the rental and his time, was most interested in a trip to Jamaica. They agreed on a fee of $10,000 for the transport of one small federal fugitive, his three overwhelmed captors, and one scared shitless blonde Señorita.

I overheard the conversation, of course. Sam said to Frank, "I have this little package here in Jamaica that needs transport to Miami, so anything you can do to help me out would be much appreciated."

Frank replied, "Of course, no *problema*, just make sure the package is secure and we'll assure safe delivery."

He said he would be there in three hours. Jamaica is not around the corner from Miami.

Brad and Hugo returned from their hunting trip around the airport with a large wooden plank, just about big enough to carry the little distraught Bahamian back to a federal prison where a term of 45 years awaited him. It took them only about five minutes to attach the bound-up little Bahamian to the wooden plank and secure him with some strips of a torn up T-shirt. So clever, these brothers of mine. I was so proud of their ingenious way of handling whatever obstacle came up.

The next three hours passed slowly, but the men had a chance to have a bit of rest and finally, Cecil, crying, sobbing and wailing, fell asleep.

Frank flew the Learjet onto the tight little runway and in a matter of minutes we were loaded aboard and up and away. The officials were so glad to see their undesirable visitors leave that they dispensed with all of the formalities and cleared the way for the Learjet to zoom away from their peaceful little island.

Goodbye to Jamaica.

The rest of the adventure was hardly that at all. The flight was smooth, quick and untroubled and at Miami International Airport we were met at a special runway by federal marshals. They welcomed little Cecil into a waiting van. Brad, ever the financial conscience of the trio, moaned a bit about the 10 grand it cost to get back from Jamaica, but finally agreed it was the only solution.

"So, what's another ten grand," Sam quipped. "The little bastard cost us a small fortune, but at least we're off the hook for a quarter mil. Case closed." And so it was.

Chapter Fifteen

J was becoming very, very determined to oust myself entirely from the bail bonds business. With the exception of super high excitement like we had bringing dear old Cecil back, I found that most of the work had become somewhat of an annoyance at best and a scary chore at the worst.

Now with some of the new investigative work I was getting, and liking, I was cutting down to a bare minimum. Bonding was becoming a little risky back in those days, mostly because of all the drug trafficking. As I said, Sammy kept me pretty secure from all of that by giving me bonds that were of lower value but had more security attached, but that was becoming more and more difficult for him, as most of his work now involved drug bonds.

I was getting tired of that too. In my investigative work, who cared if there was a bit of danger and excitement involved as long as the payoff was in dollars, not cents. And boy, did I let myself in for a surprise with some of the decisions I made in the next few weeks. Even my little island adventure did not prepare me for my next escapade.

I must digress a bit here, back to several years before, while taking the licensing course in Orlando to become a bondsman. What happened at that time very much affected my life now. I had at that time met up with some very interesting people also taking the class. It had become a prerequisite to go to the school for an 80 hour course. I had not been "grandfathered" in like Sammy had, because he had begun with bail bonds when it was still a fairly unregulated profession.

Among my classmates was a man I noticed on the first day, a long time ago. Who the hell could help noticing him? His name was Cody Williams and he had a very engaging quality. Apart from being devastatingly handsome, he exuded a charm that you could just tell would fascinate women. This guy's allure and sexual magnetism, concealed in his easy going country boy manner, whisked women off their feet, including (I was to find out much later on) some pretty sophisticated friends of mine. He was recklessly good-looking and he wore his sensuality like a fine pair of comfortable, well fitting, soft leather gloves.

Cody completed the bail bonds course but for some reason, which we never knew, did not sit for the state examination and therefore was never actually eligible for his license. I knew he was a pilot and had one or two airplanes, but I knew that only I

135

knew that because on days when he came late to class he told us bad weather flying up from Miami was the reason, and apologized in his shy and modest way. One day, after a weekend at home, I got a call late Sunday evening. It was Cody.

"Miss Lanfield," he began, "thought you might like to hitch a ride up to Orlando in the morning. I'm flying up around eight and if you and Chris would like to come along, I'd be glad to pick you all up."

I was kind of surprised, but answered, "That's kind of you, Mr. Williams. We'd love to fly up with you. What time will you get us?"

"Oh, around seven thirty would be fine, takes about a half hour to get up to my airplane at Opa Locka airport, but it sure beats a four hour drive."

"You are so right," I agreed, and he said goodbye and hung up.

Cody picked us up in his silver Lincoln Continental, a long, lean, low sweetie of a car driven by a long, lean sweetie of a guy. Only later did I find out just how low-down he could be. We parked at the airport and he gently helped us aboard. He was right, it was a quick trip and beat the crap out of sitting on the road for so many hours. Even in a Lincoln Continental.

My God, that trip was exciting. He had a little jet airplane, a Mooney, and it was a fast and very energizing experience. Very strange for me because up until then I would only fly commercial flights. How my world was rapidly changing.

We walked into class together, the three of us, and I remember some of the stares and giggles. Everyone knew I was Sam's married sister and Cody was attractive. I never saw anything to joke about where Cody was concerned. Put it down to perhaps a little bit of jealousy. Who cared, certainly not me or Chris. And Cody was way beyond that.

The class was a marvelous few weeks for me and my son, Chris, who wanted a bail bonds license and was about 21 at the time. What the hell, everyone else in the family had their licenses, he figured, why not him?

Meeting all the unusual people who were in the class was a real eye-opener and friendships were formed that have stood the test of time. Yet Cody was a real mystery man, and the mystery deepened the more I got to know him. Perhaps it was a glimpse of things to come.

Given all the facts, I really should have seen the handwriting on the wall, but who was looking? Certainly not me. I was involved with learning all this stuff related to bail bonds, studying and taking tests, and that took precedence over any social feelings that I may have possibly entertained. It was tough stuff we had to absorb.

As Sam's sister, I had to do well in the class and show interest, real progress, and, at the very least, a certain acumen. After all, it was the family business. So I did the very best I could and passed with the proverbial flying colors.

After school and all the testing was over, and licensing procedures finished, we settled down into the bail bonds business and never gave much thought to our former schoolmates. The exception, of course, was when we could share a bond in their particular county or help in the extradition or capture of a prisoner who was in their area.

I had barely settled in at home and returned to work once again, after our Jamaica jaunt, when Cody Williams called me at Sam's office. He said he had been out of the country for a few months but was back now and had a proposition for me. As I said, Cody seemed to be a secretive, enigmatic guy, so I played along with what he told me, figuring that eventually I would get the story from him. He went on and on and his seductive voice made me all the more interested, and although I had no desire for any relationship other than with my own wonderful Jack, I was very curious.

Over a few drinks at the old Speakeasy, Cody told me that a couple of criminal attorney friends of his wanted him to have a bail bonds agency and they would throw him plenty of work. His interest in me, I soon realized, was my very active and viable license. Okay. He went on to tell me there could be a lot of money in it for both of us.

"Eventually, of course, I'll take the state test and get licensed," he said to me. "However," he kind of drawled, "time is of the essence and we want to get started right away."

This was the cocaine cowboy '80s and his friends, he assured me, were right in the thick of it. I could never make a lot of money with Sam because although he did make lots of money, I was only in for 2 percent of the take and a small salary. True, Sam did most of the work, and it was obviously never intended that I would be a partner. Also, I had this thing about doing drug bonds, especially the big ones for foreign nationals, and that was where the money was. With Cody, I would be using my license and getting a full 50 percent of whatever we brought in.

"Something to think about," I said to him as he laid out the plan for me. Without my asking, he explained why he chose me as a would-be partner out of the 20 or more members of our former class.

"You're responsible and smart. I like that," he said. And, knowing him the little I did, I knew he wasn't saying it to "polish my apple." He said it sincerely, because I knew then, and was to find out even more later on, that he was a very sincere guy. Misguided, but sincere.

I did not know how misguided he actually was. His heart was in the right place but his head was pointed in the wrong direction. Unfortunately for me, and for him as well, he never told me what his real objectives and intentions were or what he was prepared to do in order to accomplish his financial goals. Or what risks lay ahead for both of us. So elated was I at the thought of making some real money for a change, meeting some important attorneys who would give us a chance at some of the fairly big bonds that were certain to be written, and having a little excitement in the offing, that I never really looked at the uncrossed t's and the undotted i's.

Cody said he would finance the entire operation, and we would be incorporated under my bail bonds license. His two airplanes, a Piper Aztec and a Mooney jet, were to remain his property, but all new assets would belong to both of us. Since it all seemed like heaven's gift to me, we soon entered into a partnership and celebrated our alliance with a champagne party for Cody and Elaine, his wife, and Jack and me. I was soon to discover that Cody loved golden champagne, golden women, and the tinkling sound of golden coins, which he collected in a big way.

I told Sammy about my new, venture and he said it was like throwing dice and could end up good or bad, winning or losing, but he knew I was anxious for change so he wished me well. But, on the other hand, he was not very happy with my move into the new bail bond office that Cody set up. There is always the possibility of competition, but, in this case, little chance of it since most of our bonds came from the northern and central parts of Florida. I knew in my heart that it was an opportunity I had to take.

Sammy had tried to set up a business for me just a week before but it would be a "name only" business and my profits would remain at 2, maybe three, percent, while my liability would grow to 100 percent. You see, in the bonds business the writer of the bond, using his "powers," which represent money, is the one responsible in case of loss and therefore must make sure he has collateral enough to pay the full face value of the bond in the event the bond is forfeited.

I discussed it with Jack at the time and we both felt that it would be, to be kind, a bit more than I wanted to handle. Sammy was a tiny bit angry with me, but as clever and innovative as he was, he was able to find some way to get yet another business open without using me. He did, of course, and then another and yet another. My brother, the super businessman.

As an added incentive, due to my increased interest in investigative work, Cody promised any investigative work that came up as a result of our bail bond ventures would belong to me. I loved that idea and when I told Sammy about it, he understood.

Shortly after all the papers were signed, and Classy Bail Bonds was born, Cody introduced me to the attorneys who were to make our fortunes for us. They were an interesting group of hotshot young criminal attorneys working out of very well-decorated law offices over on Southwest 8th Street in the section we call Little Havana. Only one of the attorneys, the nicest one, was Cuban, and he and I shared lots of café Cubanos together. And lots of secrets. Victor Suarez was a one-of-a-kind guy. He loved his work, loved Miami and loved Cody. That was one of his secrets.

I can tell it now. It was a long time ago. Victor was the friendliest of the three attorneys, and he and

I became very good friends. Every once in awhile you meet someone who is simpatico, with whom you have an immediate emotional connection. The other two guys were not nearly as interesting and now that I think of it probably had a hard time with the fact that I was a woman.

Not just a woman, but a woman bondsman who held the bail bond license. God. Eventually they got over themselves when the bonds were executed properly and their guys got out of jail in a timely fashion and with little hassle. Oh yes, I was good at what I was doing, especially when the money started rolling in. Strangely enough, a good part of the bonds were for trafficking in drugs. But they were all straight out bonds, smaller than average, and mostly written for American citizens who had stumbled onto the wrong path. Americans gone wrong.

It was very different from most of the Miami-based bonds that were written mostly for South American nationals who had just stepped off an airplane. Those were my nemesis, but the bonds up in the middle of the state were good bonds, $50,000, $60,000, $75,000 each and we got to keep the whole premium, Cody and I. Split down the middle.

A good car was first on the list for Jack and me with our new windfall. It was a first for both of us. The work was easy for Cody and me, and very enjoyable.

Maybe it's a good thing I found my work so enjoyable cause Jack and I were in for some real trouble.

Chapter Sixteen

My desire to be a rich and famous PI was burning ever bright in my heart and soul and I went back to the university to take some advanced criminology courses. Although I was not writing a lot of bail bonds anymore, I was a busy girl, having signed up with Pinkerton Security and Investigations as an intern. I wanted to learn more investigative stuff in a hands on way-and I sure did.

My teacher of sorts, Jason, a brilliant young black man with years of practical investigative experience was my "hands on guy". Let me tell you if I hadn't have loved Jack so much and feared Jason's jealous wife, there would have been a lot more hands on.

We had closed our dinner theatre show a while before, and Jack was doing solo shows all around Miami and Fort Lauderdale and making out very well. In our quest to find singing gigs for Jack, we were negotiating with a man called Uncle Solly, a wheeler-dealer agent from New York who had an office on Lincoln Road and said he was bound and determined to make Jack a star, which was fine with us. He was tied in with a local municipal judge by the name of Roy Basten who actually looked more like a small time thug than a jurist.

Roy Basten was short, fat, ugly and balding. Hey, I've nothing against balding men, some are even sexy, but when they come along with all the minus attributes this little bastard had, well, I draw the line.

It seemed that Solly and Basten figured that if they could get Jack to sign a contract, whatever happened after that could put them on the gravy train. They talked a lot, but, as I once heard some genius say, "Money talks and bullshit walks."

One Sunday morning, Jack and I went to Wolfie's, a local deli cum restaurant where all the entertainers in town congregate for bagels and lox. Actually, I preferred corned beef hash and eggs. And they made them really good, too.

About noon, we returned to the house and found that Uncle Solly had sent his chauffeur, who also doubled as a part-time hood, over to our house to "invite" us up to the office to sign the contract. Jed, the chauffeur, had scared the hell out of my daughter, Allison, and that really infuriated me. I learned a long time ago that if, in certain circumstances, you play your cards close to your chest, you can come out a winner. For that reason, neither Solly nor the judge knew what I did for a living. Basten was municipal and I really had nothing to do in that court. I much preferred the bigger cases that went state or federal. And it worked fine for me this time.

We decided, after thinking about it for awhile, to go up to the office and have a face-to-face with these guys and let them know what our feelings were. Since it was Sunday, we had planned to rest until early afternoon as there was only one performance of our show that evening. It did seem kind of strange that they wanted to have a meeting with us on a Sunday, but what the hell, show business is strange anyway. We drove over to the office on Lincoln Road.

What a glorious day it was. Early March in Miami Beach is paradise. The sky was a special cornflower blue, and, overhead, the parrots, which were always escaping from homes and from the parrot jungle way down south, were squawking their way to their favorite palm trees. Large coconuts dangled from healthy looking palms, occasionally dropping down, but always missing the lucky tourist who was passing by. Those were delightful days.

Jed, the part-time hood, part-time chauffeur, and Uncle Solly were waiting for us. No Judge Basten in sight. Out comes the contract with Solly gabbing away.

"You're gonna make it, kid, and we're gonna do it for ya," he bubbled.

"Broadway, look out, here we come, the next Big Star, no doubt about it."

He talked, we read. And read. Jack and I looked at each other and I burst out laughing.

"Are you out of your mind?" I queried. "This contract is real crap, and not even legal. Twenty years, are you kidding . . .that's bullshit."

Oh yes, I was flying.

"And where's the part," I continued, "where it says what you're going to do for Jack ...what jobs, what shows?"

Solly replied, "No guarantees in show business."

I threw the papers on the floor. Solly was turning as red as a tomato and Jed lunged for me, changed his mind, or what he had for a mind, and picked up the papers.

Jack just stood there dumbfounded.

In an instant, Solly had a gun in his hand and proceeded to give it to Jed along with the comment, "Jed, go shape up that bitch over on the Venetian Causeway, tell her I mean business, no shit, she better get her ass over here first thing in the morning if she wants to live to talk about it."

It was almost like a slow motion tableau of a bad movie. Jed moved toward the door as Solly said to Jack, "Hey, can't you keep that hairpin's mouth shut?"

I really blew my stack.

"My name is Laura, Buster, not hairpin, and, who the hell do you think you are, some stupid two bit gangster from a 1920's movie?"

"Watch it, sister," he admonished me. "You're liable to be lookin' at a whole lot of trouble."

"From who, you frigging jerk," I countered. "I presume you think you're impressing us."

146

"Well, some of the boys might impress you if you don't shut it," he said to me.

"I suppose you want us to think that you've got connections, asshole, well, you don't know what connections are, you don't know anyone, you don't even know who we know, who knows us." I was fuming.

Jack tried to calm everyone down, but I was too enraged to listen to reason. I said to Jack, "I'm getting out of here. Are you coming?"

Poor guy, he didn't know what to do.

Jack said to Solly, "Now look, don't call her names, and don't get me mad too."

I stamped my foot, another Lori-trait I got from my grandmother, Laura, for whom I was named. Works most of the time.

"I'm leaving. Jack, are you coming?"

Before he could answer, I was out the door, down the steps and halfway up the street. I walked home. It was a very long 20 blocks, and by the time I got there, my plans were made.

A long time before, maybe 15 years or so, I had gotten pretty chummy with a gal called Brandy and her bookie husband, Paulie.

Paulie had a pile of money. No one would have thought the old man had anything, but, apparently, some investments he made turned to gold and Paulie cashed out when his Dad cashed in. And it was a bundle. Turns out it allowed Paulie to change hats. From small time bookie he became big time money-lender, from money-lender he became big-time mobster. The name loan shark never quite fit this little guy, but there it was.

We stayed in touch through letters. In those days it was expensive to pick up the telephone and so we corresponded. Brandy was vague and wrote to me mostly about the good life, a pretty house and garden, nice car and good clothes. How she loved clothes. And I wrote newsy letters about my kids and my new life with Jack. When I told her about Jack and how happy I was with him, she was delighted. They had sent regrets about not coming to our wedding and although I understood, I was truly sorry that she and Paulie had not been there.

Well, getting back to that horrible day in Miami Beach, a thought washed over me. Maybe Paulie did have the connections I'd been hearing about and maybe he could help us out of this ridiculous situation. No matter what I thought about Solly and his little group, it could turn out to be dangerous for us if they actually tried to hurt us.

I had the kids to think about. When I got back to the house, I picked up the phone and on that early Sunday afternoon found out two things. First of all, that Paulie was a loyal and wonderful friend. Second, just how incredibly powerful he was in his chosen field of endeavor. He listened carefully to my tale of woe, mindful of all my sobbing and angry outbursts. He calmed me down and said that I should do nothing and that two gentlemen would come to see Jack and me and we should tell them our story. That was it.

About midnight, two very well-dressed, soft-spoken gentlemen came to our house armed with notebooks and pens and asked for the names, addresses and telephone numbers of Uncle Solly and his little gang. Jack and I told them the whole story and they politely said, "Thank you both very much." Then they left.

We never again heard from the judge, or Uncle Solly, or anyone from that entire group of losers. Never.

One night about six months later, Jack was singing at the LaRonde Room of the Fontainebleau Hotel, and as soon as he came on stage, a group of people got up from their seats and left the theatre. As they passed, I recognized Uncle Solly and a few others. Never said a word ... just left. About 10 years later I finally got some answers from Paulie about just what he said or did.

He laughed and told me.

"I just passed the word to them through some of my associates and friends that they should forget all about you both and act as if they never heard of you. Also, to cross the street if they ever saw you."

He went on. "They were most cooperative."

That was the end of that.

I always knew that my curiosity would never have been fully satisfied until he finally told us what occurred to stop those creeps from harassing us.

Our lives, our married lives, were really busy now. Jack was doing shows all over the place, New York, California, Las Vegas, and then with the meeting of two famous songwriters, Broadway loomed as a distinct possibility. A show was written for Jack and we tootled off to the Big Apple, once again to seek our fame and fortune.

The kids were older now and able to care for themselves at the house, so Jack and I felt comfortable in taking a little apartment in New York and getting ready for the forthcoming celebrity, and the fortune we expected would eventually follow. He had a legitimate offer to star in a show that, with a bit of luck, would be Broadway-bound. So we signed contracts and went into rehearsal.

In the meantime, a new song was written for Jack by a famous song-writing team and it looked like it might be a hit.

There was a successful group called the Hackers. Chick Hendry was the producer and lead singer of the group and he was going to produce and record the new song for Jack. We met him at his fancy office in the City. Hip folks never say New York, it's always "the City." So the City it was. And what an office it was, high atop Broadway, overlooking the Great White Way.

Jack was doing the recording and Chick escorted me to his private office to relax and wait. Astounding. A huge leopard-skin covered sofa, right in the center of the room, zebra skins hanging on every wall, copper-colored spears standing in front of each life-sized Zulu warrior, feathers, painted faces and all, and a black shag carpet you could get lost in if you were a pygmy. All those platinum records on the wall were startling. One could get blinded from the glare. A lovely bottle of Dom Perignon was chilling its little self in a gold plated wine cooler. Was I impressed? I still don't know. I was something.

Chick said he would open the bottle of Champagne.

"Have you ever had Dom Perignon?" he inquired.

"Yes," I replied, "I like it with a peach in it."

Uh-oh. Wrong thing to say.

"You're the peach, this time, honey," he purred.

The handwriting was on the bottle. Discovering myself to be not quite as sophisticated as I thought made me a little uncomfortable. Falling ungracefully onto the lush carpet from my little pedestal of unreality was a crushing blow, but even before I hit the proverbial floor I knew I was in over my head. A real smooth casting couch producer was more than I could handle and I found myself racing through all my smart ad-lib remarks and coming up empty.

So I simply said to this slick asshole, "I don't do that, I'm married to Jack." Not good enough. Insults came like rapid gunfire.

""Who the fuck do you think you are, the Virgin Mary? This is the fuckin' '80s," he admonished me. "Everyone does it, everyone, that is everyone who wants their husband to have a hit record, sweetie."

All I could think was, *I've gotta get out of here.*

151

There would have been no percentage in arguing the point with this semi-insane sex maniac, so I picked myself up and trekked through his almost ankle-deep carpeting and exited the scene. Take two.

Jack found me in the waiting room and we said our goodbyes to everyone. I never said a word until we got back to our hotel and then I looked into his clear blue eyes and told my dear husband about the brutish producer of hit records and his tyrannical attempted "hit" on me, as a precursor for a hit for Jack.

We laughed like hell. We laughed at Chick, at me, at Jack, and at both of us for not anticipating this craziness.

The show opened and Jack was wonderful in it, but a poor script and lousy music spoiled things and he never made Broadway. Not that time, at least.

Chapter Seventeen

*T*ripping down to the women's jail was not my most unfavorite thing – can't say I loved it at 3 or 4 a.m., but it beat the hell out of the men's jail facility.

I had no choice, actually. Cody said to write the "girlie" bonds, so I did. It was noisy with the feminine ring of indignation at the booking process, the bawdy guards, the antiseptic smells, the whole thing. Couldn't blame them, these "innocent in their minds" women dragged like refuse from the sanctity of their jobs – albeit on the street – to the incredible lunacy at the women's jail.

A 4 a.m. lockup meant I could expect to leave the jail about 6 or 7 and drive home or to the office through the golden sunrise beginning of another incredible tropical South Florida day.

It was never a problem. We wrote all the ladies' bonds from the Booby Trap. Cody knew the owners, a couple of tough lesbians, Lita and Cheetah. Ruby was the sweetest, exotic dancer Cody and I had ever met. Blond, 30ish, divorced with a little son. She liked Miami Beach and I often saw her in the afternoon with her young boy, walking the beach. She was so damn demure and Sunday school teacher-like, no one could ever know she was a stripper in one of the hottest, toughest clubs in Miami.

After we took her out on bond for the third time, she kind of adopted me. She said she didn't have any good friends and was hesitant to get too friendly with some of the real tough other dancers. Her Arab ex-husband had long since gone back to his country and she was very much alone.

It was the early '80s and my kids were teenagers and it was refreshing to have a child around. She often came over to my house after she left the beach and with her baby, they'd have milk and cookies. I always enjoyed a late afternoon Café Con Leche and then when they left, I'd have a delicious little nap.

One early evening while I was at home, I got a call from Ruby, who told me that she'd been arrested in Key West the night before and wanted to know if I would come and bond her out. I had no problem writing bonds in Monroe Country and even though the bond was only $1,000, I said I'd be there.

Ruby said, "I know that it's just a small bond but I'd really appreciate your coming down to get me.

154

Some of the other girls at the club have arranged bail with this really sleazy guy from down here but I'm -"

"Don't worry about it, Ruby." I said. "Nothing's planned for the evening anyway."

She thanked me and I told her I'd be there by 8 or 9 o'clock.

I called Cody and he said, "Okay, write it, Lori. She's a good kid."

Ordinarily I'd never drive 175 miles to write a $1000 bond, but this was a special case.

I knew that a lot of the strip girls often went out of the county to pick up a job, but Ruby had a sweet deal at the Trap and the two owners liked her and went out of their way to be nice to her. I know they loved her baby because at Christmas they had sent a basket of goodies and baby clothes, which Lita told me they shopped for at Sak's, and had a hell of a good time doing it. I wondered to myself as I drove down what made her take a job in one of the Key West spots. Most of them were sleazy and kind of run down. They must have offered her some really good incentive, probably money. That WAS the universal solvent, the green wonder that made the wheels go 'round and 'round.

The traffic was fairly light heading south at that time of the evening until the Seven Mile Bridge where it usually bottle-necked. After that it was stop and go until we finally came to the golden city of Key West. The Pink Sunset Club was a bit west of the beach in a part of town dotted with sleazy bars and 10th rate motels with names like the Kookey Kaktus and the Flaming Flamingo. If it weren't for low class there'd be no class. What part of that crap did I not understand?

The parking lot at the Pink Sunset was practically full. All out of state license plates, I noted. But hell, it was mid-season so all the snowbirds were here, and from what I saw, a few snowflakes as well. We had coined that term to describe some of the gay women who had snow-white skin from never going out in the daytime. Some of them wore sunglasses as big as saucers to cover up their light-sensitive eyes. Oh yes, *el sol* can be a dangerous commodity. There were four of them in the parking lot when I parked. No sunglasses. No midnight burn.

I stopped by the club first before going to the little jail on the other side of town. The reason being that I wanted to talk to the club manager, whom I had met on one prior occasion. At the time, I was not there to write a bond but rather to offer Cody's and my services in case he needed a bond written in Miami. It was the year before and although we'd never heard from him, I kind of thought we might someday.

Alex Barrios was in his office, a portly gentleman in his late 50s, balding, very Latino. His welcoming gesture was to take the fucking Cohiba out of his mouth and plant a wet, cigary kiss on my cheek. God, how I felt like wiping it clean but knew that would be most inappropriate. Smiling, he said, as I flashed my business card, "I remember *you*, Missy. How could I ever forget such lovely ..." and his eyes dropped to my chest, "hair," he continued and smiled.

Okay, Sucker, I thought, *Play it your way.* And as an addendum, *Don't you see enough tits?*

Of course, this was all tacitly played out. I, of course, had far too much class to engage in such banter.

"So, Miss Ruby is your gal." He puffed, "Over at the jail," he said and nodded his head in an easterly direction, "So silly, cops see a new ass, pardon me, a new face and they go a little wild. She was doing nothing out of the ordinary. They just did a sweep, maybe her pasties were on wrong, who knows, just part of the game. A few bucks in their coffers. Nothing to worry about."

"I'm hardly worried, long drive for a thousand-buck bond though, and she will appear," I assured him, "so they really won't get much of that. If that's what they're after."

Back in my car I followed the road over to the beach and the jail. No women's jail here, everybody, all the folks, men and women lumped together in a small building. In years to come, this would change, but for now this was it.

Not noisy like the Miami-Dade County jails. There was a kind of hush to the atmosphere. Checking with the duty guard was a simple matter of entering the front gate and showing my credentials. The heavy metal door clinked open.

"You here for who?" the female guard asked.

"Ruby McKinnen," I responded. She checked her chart.

"No McKinnen here," she offered, then added, "She have an AKA?"

157

I thought for a brief moment, "Yes, Pearl. Ruby Pearl."

She chuckled, "We got her, Ma'am. Sounds like a real jewel of a gal."

Funny thing, she said it kind of matter of fact-like, no sarcasm intended.

I smiled and said, "Where is she?"

I followed the guard into the very limited inner sanctum of the Key West jail, and there was Ruby with her back to us, talking to another inmate in an unlocked cell. I overheard a bit of her conversation.

"Yes, she will be here. We're kind of friends-only lady bondsman I ever met and believe me, she is a lady."

"Thanks." I loud-whispered and Ruby turned around and looked at me.

I was shocked at her appearance. Her long blond hair was pulled back in a ponytail and it was obvious that she had a blackened left eye.

From the arrest? I wondered. *Hardly*, I countered to myself, *Key West police are not violent and would certainly not be in a pussy-raid.*

"Well, now that we know what a gem I am, Miss Ruby, perhaps you can introduce me to your friend and tell me what the fuck happened to your eye. Funny, Barrios did not mention it."

The tough-looking gal talking to Ruby said, "Hi, I'm Roberta, pleased to meetcha."

She extended her hand. She had long black satin gloves on and a couple of large but obviously faux diamond rings on over her glove. I shook her hand and looked into her eyes. We bondsmen are really good at looking at eyes. Her eyes were full of secrets, intense, dark and liquid like pools of inky black oil. Her lips were pouty and very full as if they'd been pumped up with some cosmetic yet unknown to our everyday world. The eyebrows were thin and highly arched as if Joan Crawford had drawn a pattern across her swarthy forehead. Roberta's hair was short and very dark brown, almost black, with a shocking wave of shimmering silver about an inch inside from over her right eye across to her left ear lobe. Dramatic.

But I knew at a glance that Roberta was really Robert. Maybe his balls were gone but his manhood was very much in evidence. Navy blue glints on his chin, probably after a long night in jail, gave it all away. Who the fuck cared?

We'd probably never see her again. But one never knew, did one? I decided to be real nice to this person. After all, she seemed to be sympathetic to Ruby and that made her A-okay in my book.

I invited Roberta to come and visit with us in Miami and maybe go out on the town one weekend. She never did, but much later on I was really glad I made that decision. Actually, Roberta told me she lived on a nearby Key and rarely visited Miami.

Most important at that moment was getting Ruby out and back to Miami. Luckily, the women who cared for her son, Chris, lived upstairs from Ruby and kept him safely all hours of the day or night. It wasn't lost on me that her son and my son had the same name and sometimes I tripped out on the nostalgic beat of the similar drum.

159

The bonding details were done in less than an hour, and soon Ruby and I were in my car on our way back to Miami. There was no traffic at midnight and as we drove, I tried to think of a way to get Ruby to explain her battered face without seeming too nosy. Of course, as her bondsman, I was certainly entitled to know. Actually, since she was delivered to my care, custody and control I was essentially responsible for her well-being, at least more or less. And as my friend, she should have no reluctance in telling me the details of how her very pretty eye got so banged up.

We drove in silence. Ruby knew I had a big thing about not smoking in my car or around me in general and she was quite cooperative, although I had the feeling she was dying for a cigarette. When we got to Key Largo, I knew there was a night restaurant called the Caribbean Club, so I pulled off the road and she got out of the car. It always amazed me that smokers could pull out a cigarette, light up, draw a few puffs and put the cigarette out, all in less than a minute. She did. Satisfied, she smiled, whispered me a thanks and we went into the restaurant.

The night was blown, I'd never sleep anyway, so what the hell. I ordered a cup of *café Cubano*. Thank God for the Latin culture that delightfully invaded our culinary environment.

Ruby joined me by ordering a *café con leche* and since we both had no dinner, some *papas relenos*, these wonderful potato balls stuffed in the middle with a fragrant and spicy bit of savory meat and then fried to perfection, a real treat for less than a buck. We had two each, a *pastelito,* and a *guava con queso* rounded out our midnight snack, and we both felt a lot better. Which is why it surpised the hell out of me when Ruby started crying as we walked out to the car, "You're so good, Lori," she wailed. "Came all this way to get me, find me all beat up and never mention a word."

I interrupted, "Figured if I waited, you'd tell me in your own good time, and there was no rush. You're not going anywhere, right? Remember, Ruby, it's all only a game anyway."

"You'd better believe it, only came down here because Crystal, one of the gals where I work, said I'd make a basic three hundred fifty dollars plus at least that in tips for the night. She was right, I did. Barrios paid me up front and the tips rolled in all night."

She paused, obviously to think and put her facts in chronological order.

"Everything was fine until about 3 a.m.," she began, "and since it was a five o'clock closing, I figured I could count on another hundred at least. The crowd was hot, Friday nights are good. Lots of singles of course, but I was surprised to see at least a dozen couples as well. Sometimes the women get so turned on it surprises the hell out of me. A few gay gals, but most of them were straight couples ready to party. Four of them whispered in my ear, but since my baby was born I don't go that route. Know what I mean?" she asked as she raised an eyebrow.

"Yeah, Ruby. I didn't just fall off the turnip truck, the same tricks are old hat. Never can tell by looking at folks what turns them on and rings their bells and spins their suds."

"Don't I know it." She smiled.

It was nice to see her smile but I knew there was a lot more to come. Suddenly, like a dam bursting, the tears came flowing out.

"He seemed so nice, wanted a private dance and all, and then suddenly, right after the lap dance, he punched me in the eye," she paused, "but that was not really the worst of it. It was what he said. What he said," she repeated. "And then he ran out. He had given me a hundred bucks and seemed to enjoy what I was doing and then he flipped and ..."

"Ruby," I said, "What did he say and what did he look like and did anyone in the club know him?"

He said, " 'For the love of Allah' just before he struck me. And Lori, he was very handsome about forty, dark Latin-looking serious big brown eyes, clean shaven about six feet tall, nice Armani suit."

"Hey wait a minute here, that's a great description. You could be a detective for Chrissake."

I chuckled, trying to break the tension.

"Yes, detective. How come I did not detect what he was about to do? Anyway, everyone was in shock, happened so fast and in a darkened corner of the club. He took off very quickly and although several of the men ran out to the parking lot, all they saw was a silver car screeching out of the lot. And, stranger still, no license plate. None."

She got very quiet.

"It was a set-up." I said.

She nodded.

"I mean the whole fuckin' thing, bringing you down here away from the safety of your club and Lita and Cheetah, Christ, those gals would have cut his balls off."

"I know." Ruby whispered.

"So do you also know who set it up, who the hell would hate you that much?"

The answer was in her eyes. Sad, blue eyes shining now with sparkling tears that ran down her cheeks. Ruby waited a long minute and then said, "It had to be him, Hassan. He wants my baby but the law is on my side. He is not an American and I am a good mother!" she sobbed. "I know this was just a warning from him."

We got back on the road and in about an hour we were back in Miami on our way to the beach. Once again the beauty of a typical sunrise overwhelmed me as we drove East over the MacArthur Causeway into the dazzling brightness of the new day.

Ruby was exhausted and so was I. So after agreeing to meet late in the afternoon, we parted so we could both get some well-deserved rest. It's a long trip to make in one night down to Key West and back and certainly not one that I would enjoy making very often.

As fate would have it I only did it one more time, but the terror that was involved made that trip live on in my dreams and waking moments almost until this very day.

Chapter Eighteen

*R*uby did not come over that afternoon and I did not see her again for a week. I understood that she had to cool off after that terrible misadventure so I did not call her, and since things were quiet at the club where she worked, I kind of left things alone. Big mistake.

A notice requesting Ruby's appearance in court arrived the next week with a date set for the following month. I knew she would be notified as well, so I did not call her.

I was really busy with bonds around that time. Cody was flying up to Okeechobee quite a bit. I preferred staying at the office we kept over on Miami's northeast side near Little Haiti and the railroad tracks. Interesting place!

He would meet the client in Okeechobee or the Tampa Bay area, then fly me up to write the bond, and then back to Miami.

Since I had not seen Ruby or her baby in a couple of weeks, I dropped by the club one night about 11. Things were in full swing as usual and there seemed to be a hell of business that night. The dimly lit atmosphere was typical of strip clubs the world over. Low lights, bits of soft-colored neon glowing here and there, and shiny silver poles lifting mindlessly into the air from a small black stage. The bar was covered in an exotic animal print, purple and black. The barstools were soft purpley fleece and extended all the way around the horseshoe-shaped bar. There was perfume in the air, heavy and very sexy as it mingled with the sweet pungent odor of feminine perspiration.

A girl was setting up on her pole, the pulsating thump thump of her recorded music beginning to fill the room as her much anticipated act began. Dressed in a silver filagree bra and shorts with long silver gloves, this bronzed beauty with raven hair down to her hips began a slow movement around her pole, one leg bent at the knee and draped around the pole, the other on the stage. She began to move her hips in an up and down movement as she slowly removed one glove. I guessed the other was soon to follow, as well as mostly every other article of clothing, so I did a hasty disappearing act behind the haze of shimmering purple curtains and I was in the inner sanctum of the club.

Ruby had just finished a set and was in the crowded dressing room. I knocked and went in and she came over and gave me a big hug. Here eyes were healed and she looked really rested and very vivacious. We walked outside to the bar and sat down. I could see several men throwing appreciative glances in her direction. Of course, I got a few hungry stares as well. I was glad I had all my clothes on. Made me just a little nervous to see all that raw sexual energy, so obvious- the room was heavy with it.

Wise up, kid, I said to myself. *This isn't a church for fuck's sake.*

But the blue heaviness so engulfed me that I broke out in a sweat and Ruby noticed.

Laughing her tinkly little giggle, she said, "Lori, loosen up. They don't bite. Remember what you told me, 'It's all a game.' So play it easy, hon."

I had to laugh in agreement, and then my frazzled psyche settled down.

"So," I began, "court date next week. You okay with that? Your kid arranged?"

She looked at me with those big blue eyes and I thought I caught a glint of fear, but she said, "Sure, all set. Are you going to drive us or should I try to get a ride?"

"No need. I'll drive. At least it won't be a midnight run again. Let's leave about 8 a.m. The hearing is at 11."

Never for one moment did I think that it would be anything but a single easy trip down to Key West. An early morning glide down to a short court date which undoubtedly would bring a quick dismissal of the charges, and we'd have lunch somewhere and be home by 6.

I can't believe I was so naïve.

166

The music was getting louder and the heavy blue was back again, and I knew it was time for my hasty exit.

"Night, Ruby." I managed as I slid off the purpley fur covered barstool and made my way to the front exit. My car was with Josh, the carhop. I flipped him a fiver and up came my little gold chariot.

And off I went to my castle, my real world.

I wondered how come I had not seen Ruby and the baby around the beach, wondered, but only for a moment. Tired, I crawled into bed beside a sleepy Jack who gave me a tired hug, clicked the TV off, rolled over and fell asleep. This late business was not too good for my sex life. But we managed nonetheless. We had been together a long time now and the magic was still there.

Early the next morning after my cup of that sweet *café Cubano* I so craved, the phone rang. It was Cody. He said he needed to talk to me and would I meet him at the office?

"On my way," I quipped and he knew that meant he'd see me in about an hour. Which he did.

"Something I need to discuss with you, Lori, about the dancer, Ruby," Cody smiled, but his voice had a worry in it, which I picked up immediately.

"What's up?"

"Well, tell me what's up with her. What happened to her in Key West?"

I cut him off with, "She got arrested. It was a stupid and uncalled for pussy raid and she ..."

"No," he raised his voice, "what happened to her? Who blacked her eye and was he found?"

"We don't know and no, to my knowledge he was never found. I heard some funny stuff from Lita and Cheetah."

"So did I." He interrupted.

"The ex-husband is an Arab and when the guy slugged her he mentioned Allah. Do you think there's a connection?" I asked.

"Yes, without a doubt. So be really careful when you drive down with her next week."

He paused and rubbed his chin as he put the rest of his thoughts together.

"Perhaps I should come down there with you in case of any problem."

"Nah, Cody, thanks, but I can handle it. I'll have my gun and I'm really not worried."

Cody seemed content with that and as he uncurled himself from the tobacco leather office chair and stood up I realized for the thousandth time what a gorgeous hunk he was.

Sexy, son of a bitch if I weren't so in love with Jack, well … I stopped my thoughts there.

The week passed quickly, and at 8 a.m. the next Friday, Ruby appeared on my doorstep. She was dressed in a pale yellow jumpsuit with embroidered white daisies on the collar and cuffs. Her shiny blond hair was caught up in a ponytail with a white daisy clip holding it in place. She never looked like who she really was and one would never know where we were really going or why. Well, that's show business. We got in my car for the long drive and although she did not speak, Ruby seemed very nervous. I sensed that she felt we were being followed and was very frightened by the sense of impending danger.

I reflected on my talk with Cody and wondered as I left why the hell he was taking such a personal interest in this Ruby situation.

I decided to do my own investigation to find out as much as I could about her ex-husband and what I found out really shocked me. This husband of hers, Hassan, was no ordinary Muslim, if there ever is such a thing as an ordinary anybody. But, having several Muslim friends who live here in Miami, some in New York and a few families in London, I know that what they have in common is that they all keep a fairly low profile. They live simple lives, and I must say they have taught me a lot about the very interesting Muslim culture.

It appeared that the enigmatic Hassan's far-reaching tentacles were powerful enough to integrate into our world with a possible threat to even the likes of Cody.

But I paid it little mind. I can get very paranoid at times, so I sort of put it on the back burner for the moment. I really had no idea of the imminent danger that awaited us.

Chapter Nineteen

By 10:30 we were in Key West. We drove over to the city hall on Whitehead Street and went into the courthouse.

That fat balding club manager, Barrios, was there with Roberta, no cigar and a fine assortment of rather demurely dressed exotic dancers. Funny, I thought, the very friendly Roberta barely looked at us. Oh, well.

"Hell of a raid," I said to Ruby, who nodded in agreement.

Up until that moment, I never imagined that the whole thing was obviously planned to frighten, intimidate and embarrass Ruby. Who on earth could set up such a thing? What power did such a person have, and why would he use it in this way? I was soon to find out the hard way.

The bailiff called the court. The judge rapped a few gavel raps and court was in session. Two uniformed police officers twitched nervously in the front row and the seedy local bondsman who represented five of the six defendants smiled a slimy smile. Bastard, he made a good night's pay, $500 for 10 minutes of his sleazy time. Not that I resented his earnings. Christ, I was in the same business and our office did take $100 to get Ruby out. No, it was his shit-eating grin that offended me.

"Look at all the pussy I got," he seemed to be intimating. And I found that offensive.

One by one, the girls got up before the bench and one by one their cases were dismissed. No excuses, no reason, no lack of prosecution. The cops were there. Just over, that's all. Then it was Ruby's turn. Seemed the judge saved the best of that particular case for last. I walked forward with Ruby, as her bondsman, and with no attorney present I was entitled to do that. The judge looked at us, raised his gavel and said, "Guilty - $500 fine. Next!"

So who got to that rat bastard? I wondered.

She was no more guilty than any of the others and they were really guilty of nothing more than plying their trade. Justice is served.

We walked back to our seats and I asked Ruby if she had the money, still in friggin' shock over the ridiculous outcome of this travesty.

"Yeah," she said, "figured this might happen. After all, I'm the out-of-towner."

Could she really be so naïve? I wondered and stared at her. But I knew it would be better to say nothing.

171

But my mind was running away with the unfairness of it all and I wondered what the real reason for the guilty verdict could be. Again, I came back to the only truth that could have made this happen.

This judge was as crooked as a crippled centipede wiggling down the path. No sense to it at all. Or was there? Of course it made perfect sense. Whoever set this up wanted it played out his way. And it was.

Cody must have had an inkling of what was going on. But I thought he was safely back at our office in Miami. His utter and total concern was evident when we walked outside to the parking lot and he was standing there.

"Get in the car now." He said to me. "You too, Ruby," he said in a very unfamiliar voice, and there was no humor in the way he looked, either.

Cody always drove a new Cadillac convertible. Something about bondsmen and Caddies. Me, I went for a car that was not all flash.

We got in and he drove silently to the other side of town, away from the Beach. That we were headed to the small airport was evident.

Parking, he told us that he had rented a small Beachcraft four-seater, pointed in the direction of a red and white airplane. He told us to board. We did and as he crossed the tarmac to the airport office to make final arrangements and probably file a flight plan, my whole being began to shake with an unprecedented fear.

172

Seated in the copilot seat, I made sure that Ruby, who was seated just behind me, was settled and buckled up. Then I got up and started to make my way down the small set of stairs I had just climbed up. As I held on to the railing, I noticed a Lincoln Continental pull up close to where Cody was. He was walking toward us when suddenly a single shot rang out and he was hit and down on the tarmac in an instant.

"God, no," I screamed but before I could move, two guys from the front seat of the Lincoln got out of the car. They ignored Cody as he lay on the ground and came up the steps of the airplane.

One of them grabbed my arm and yanked me down the steps.

"All right, girlie," the uglier of the two barked at Ruby who was still inside the airplane. "Up and out of there now! Or you'll get the same as him."

And so Ruby unbuckled her seatbelt and followed him down the steps.

Seconds later we were in the Lincoln and squealing tires pulled us away from the airport and parking lot and Cody, who seemed to be hanging on for dear life.

Chapter Twenty

J was mortified. I kept thinking as my mind's eye held captive the picture of Cody lying on the ground dying or maybe dead. What an ignominious way for this brave soldier of fortune to die, on the black, sooty tarmac of a lonely airport in Key West.

My mind wandered to a thousand places. On so many of our long flights to different parts of Florida to write bonds, Cody had told me, without boasting or ego-ing up, of his experiences as a young derring-do pilot bringing others to safety from disaster in other parts of the country and the world.

Get a grip. I nearly said aloud but it was to myself, and I whispered softly to myself again, "No time now for ephemeral bullshit."

My handbag was hanging from my left shoulder in a sort of tucked up position since I was sitting down in the large and comfy leather backseat of the Lincoln Continental. I moved over closer to a now weeping Ruby as the two men in the front seat spoke to each other in a language I recognized as Arabic. The gutteral sounds cut through me like a knife. I was silent, thinking of how I could remove my .38 from the recesses of my leather specially constructed handbag. It had been a gift years ago from my brother Brad and came in handy when I needed to conceal a weapon.

The men were definitely Muslim and the driver by far the younger of the two. They both had very black hair and mustaches. The younger of the two kept looking back at us nervously and somehow I felt that this was probably his first caper. Be that as it may. First, last or otherwise, we were in the shit. Trying to be as inconspicuous as possible, I sidled even closer to Ruby and winked hoping that she'd figure out that I was trying to do something important for both of us. Very important. If it worked, it would save our fuckin' lives.

The driver was yacking away and seemed a bit distracted. I guess he figured Cody was on the ground miles away and we were safe in the back seat of his car. What could go wrong?

Wrong. I carefully managed to remove my little gun from the bag and put it in my bra, that's right, 38 to 38. Something to be said for not being flat-chested, for having a bra size that covers two Zip codes. The cold metal against my breast felt very

175

reassuring and with a smile I was able to comfort Ruby a little bit. She visibly relaxed.

I had no idea where we were. The car was moving very fast up U.S. 1 heading north. Palm trees blurred as we passed them and it had started to rain. A slow, gray drizzle that beat a gentle rat-a-tat-tat on the windshield as we drove. I tried in vain to look for something - a mile marker, anything - out there on the road that would tell me where we were.

Nothing I recognized. The short, irate toot of a trailer tractor as we passed clearly defined that we were going too fast. Hoped our driver had his safe driver certificate in the friggin' glove compartment. He had to slow down because the rain was getting heavier and the monotonous whoosh-whoosh sound of the windshield wipers was apparently making the guy in the passenger seat nervous. He started to speak loudly, more Arabic, with a little English thrown in "Slow down" I recognized. Older and probably a little smarter, he did not want to end up squashed like a bug by the side of the road.

We were both practically cuddled in the backseat when suddenly I saw something I recognized. We were leaving one Key and getting on to another. The sign said Long Pine Key. We were about 30 miles north of Key West.

The driver pulled off the road onto the ocean side making a sharp right turn onto a small dirt road with stands of palmetto palms on both sides. I ticked off time with my mind focused on how far we would be from U.S. 1. About four minutes later, we came to an abrupt stop. Ruby flew off the big white leather seat and hit her face on the back of the driver's seat.

That was when Mr. Young, as opposed to Mr. Old, noticed my handbag and snatched it from me. Good old Zip code boobs!

The driver motioned to Ruby to hand over her little purse as well. She did. No argument from us. These bastards, whoever they were, meant business.

Soon after we stopped, the driver got out of the car, opened our door and motioned to Ruby and me to get out. He did not speak. Seemed to me he was a bit embarrassed by his broken English and he sure as hell could not speak to us in Arabic, or so I thought.

The man in the passenger's seat got out and called to Ruby, "*Muráh kalil-et el haya.*"

He said this as he partially opened the door to the house. Then he went over to the side of the house to talk to the other man. I could not hear what they were saying.

The day was getting gloomier by the minute. A gray, hazy rain was falling and I looked at my watch and was surprised to see that it was only 3 o'clock. It was going to be a long day. Even though it was still fairly early, the sky had darkened and it almost looked like night was upon us. The house was the bungalow style so popular in the Keys and had small coconut palms heavily laden with coconuts all around the perimeter of the compact little home. Brilliant purple bougainvillea blossomed in all its majestic glory and contrasted nicely with the white wooden shingles and terra cotta roof tiles.

I looked over at Ruby and she appeared to be terribly upset by the words spoken by the Muslim guy. I raised a quizzical eyebrow.

"Nothing, don't worry. He just called me a bad name," she said.

"But, how did you …?"

She interrupted me, "I speak Arabic fluently. I lived in Saudi Arabia for several years when I was married and before Chris was born. My husband Hassan owned a theatre and I first came there as part of an American Ballet Company, just one of many places I danced as part of a tour."

She sighed deeply and went on, "Yes, I was a professional ballet dancer."

She looked around. The two men were standing and talking by the doorway to the house where we were parked.

"Don't worry, they don't know much English," she said, "and if we talk fast they'll never understand."

"Who gives a shit what they understand? What I can't understand is this whole friggin' situation."

I was a bit agitated, no doubt. Tired, hungry, distressed, worried about Cody, to name just a few of my tangled emotions.

As we stood by the partly open front door, Ruby went on with her story. "When I left Hassan and took the baby home to America, it was supposed to be just for a visit."

Her look darkened. "I never, ever planned to go back to him."

"So why didn't you go back to the ballet. Seems a hell of a lot more ..."

"Decent?" She cut in.

"Well," I said, kind of embarrassed.

"Well, it is. But Hassan saw to it that I could never get a job with my old company and ballet is a small world and he has powerful influences. I dance. Now I am an exotic dancer. Simple as that. We do what we have to do." She said that with an energy that I had not seen her exhibit before.

"Okay. I've got the picture. I never thought any less of you because of your job but it must have been one hell of an adjustment."

"It was."

"I can just imagine the whole scenario. Young, American, beautiful, talented, married to an Arab, probably living a luxurious life, dreamlike I guess."

"Right," she nodded.

"So what happened?"

"You'd have to be there to understand. In a nutshell, he only married me to have a child, a son and thus one foot in the good old U.S.A. An American citizen son, the dream of many Arabs. I could go on and on and tell you of all the horrible experiences, all the devastating insults and the means Hassan used to humiliate and belittle me. To own me mind, body and soul was his aim.

"He was an unusual and violent man. Even his family seemed to be on my side and take issue with the abuse, but there was nothing they could do about it."

179

Suddenly, the older man beckoned to us to come into the house. He held the front door wide open and we both climbed the stairs and went inside. The musty smell was overpowering. It was dark inside and I could feel the dampness rising to meet us.

Having no idea what these guys had planned for us, I naturally thought the worst. But whatever, there was nothing, not a goddamn thing I could do about it. At least not then. I had learned long before that it was not a good idea for a woman to get into physical combat with a man if she could avoid it. Even if they were small and wiry, which these two were definitely not, it would be bad for the woman. Has to do with musculature and a certain male-directed energy, which for the most part, women don't possess. That's why we have such fine-tuned minds, even if we happen to be blond. Some would disagree.

The problem intensified when the younger of the two men motioned to us to go into the bedroom and sit on the bed.

Uh-oh, I thought, *could this be what it's all about?*

When he spoke slowly, his English was understandable enough. I followed Ruby into the bedroom and as I did so, I saw through the doorway the older, and heavier of the men go through our handbags. Then they followed us into the bedroom, looked around and left.

Nothing sucker, I chuckled to myself.

A couple of wallets, some lipsticks, loose change and that was it. Again, thank God for my 38s.

The bedroom was cool and smelled like it had been closed up for a long time. They left the door to the bedroom open. I heard them speaking on their mobile telephone but could not understand what they were saying. I checked the jalousie window and it was locked up tighter than a bug's rear end. Hard to slip out of jalousies anyway, unless you are a snake.

My mind began to race as the conversation in the other room seemed to be heating up, and I said to Ruby, "For Chrissake, what are they saying?"

"Well," she hesitated and then said, "They were waiting for instructions from someone but they have not had any communication from them."

"Probably because out here in the boonies the mobile phones have trouble."

"Is that an educated guess?" she queried.

"Yeah, but probably very accurate."

Suddenly, it got very quiet in the other room and I got a really queasy, uneasy feeling in the pit of my stomach. About two hours had passed since we first went into the house, and since it was getting dark outside, and inside too since there were no lights in the house, I was really getting nervous.

I rarely find myself without a Plan B, but my mind was blank and Ruby certainly wasn't helping any by beginning to sob again. The older of the two men, whom the other had referred to as Adji, came into the bedroom and told us we were leaving the house.

What a fuckin' waste of time this is, I thought to myself. *Seems that things have gone very badly for our two lads. Looks like either they have a Plan B or they are really fucked up.*

I was totally and utterly confused.

As we walked outside into the darkness, the shrubbery thick all around us, I wondered if either of the men had with him the gun they had used to shoot Cody. From the little that I saw, it was a handgun. Not a small one like mine, but certainly not a rifle or some such.

I knew one thing for certain - we must not get back in that car, for if we did we would really be in danger. Their tempers were getting short and I sensed that they pretty much did not care what happened to us, so long as they could get away clean.

Ruby whispered to me, as we walked side by side in the murky shadows of the night, that she thought she overheard one of them just say that they might have to kill us since their communications were long overdue and it was becoming increasingly dangerous for them to keep us. Muslim or not, apparently they knew the kidnapping laws and murdering us seemed a better option. We were safer to them dead than alive! Not a very comforting thought. Ruby was becoming more nervous and agitated and suddenly like a streak of yellow daisy-covered lightning she bolted and ran in the opposite direction from the car. Into the darkness she ran and soon disappeared into the shadowed shrubs.

Chapter Twenty-One

Both men ran after her and so I ran after them.

What the hell could I do? To leave her alone was unthinkable even though I was scared shitless. I could imagine what she was feeling.

I had the shuddering thought wash over me that Ruby knew we would be killed when we were kidnapped. That she knew that her ruthless ex-husband would then get her kid. No questions asked. We all know what mothers are capable of when their children are threatened. So she ran. In a short minute I heard a terrible scream, a man's scream, a scream of horrible pain and fear all mingled together. In the pale, hazy falling-rain moonlight I was able to see the figure of a man, the younger man. He must have tripped and fallen over the coral rock, ripping his flesh as he toppled downward into the dark, swirling waters below. He was struggling but it seemed to no avail.

Ruby was screaming and I immediately saw that the older, dark, swarthy man, Adji, had his hands around her throat. I called out to him to stop, but he just cursed me in that gutteral voice of his and the moonlight offered me just enough light to see them struggling. I did the only thing I could. One quick flash as a single shot rang out and Ruby fell to the ground like a sack of potatoes. She was released from Adji's grip the moment the slug tore into his body. True, it was dark and I had only the moonlight to guide me, and it was a long shot, but he was big, a good target. And I am a good shot.

God, I didn't want to do it. What a jolt went through me when the recoil from my .38 and the sharp retort of the round registered on me. Like a slow-mo movie I dropped my left hand to my side, placed my .38 in the waistband at the back of my snug-fitting jeans, and moved forward toward Ruby.

And obviously Adji wasn't following us anymore. I no longer heard any splashing from the waters below the sea wall. Either the young man had been swept down the rough, turbulent murky waters or he had found a way to swim to shore. If that were the case, I reckoned, we were still in danger.

Ruby still sitting on the ground rubbing her neck, lifted her head and motioned to me that she was all right. I knelt down beside her and we had a very silent moment.

"You saved my life," she rasped. "Do you have any idea what it felt like? His big hands were tightening around my throat and I couldn't breathe, I couldn't see, oh Lori, I was so scared."

"Ruby," I said gently as I could, "try not to think about that now. We have to get the hell out of here. Remember, he was on the mobile phone and others, who knows who, know where we are."

I stood and moved over to the very still Adji and choking back an overwhelming desire to vomit, reached into first his shirt and then his pants pockets to see if I could find the car keys. No luck, they must be either in or out of the water with the other guy. In any case, I would not have them or the use of that lovely Lincoln Continental.

"No time to waste," I whispered to Ruby, and she was on her feet in a minute.

"Hold onto my hand," I said, and we navigated the tropical foliage on the path and moved very quickly onto the dirt road. I did not really feel safe, only relieved to be on our own. It had started to rain again, a cold, heavy drizzle, and very soon we were both soaked to the skin.

We kept walking towards U.S. 1 and although it seemed like it was taking forever because the narrow road was all twisty and turny and now muddy from the incessant rain, I knew we were making progress and would soon be at the highway. We were exhausted and huffed and puffed every step of the way. We knew somehow, some way, we'd have to hitch a ride.

There were no cars and no people on the road behind us, which meant that the driver of the Lincoln was either dead or disabled, so that was one worry off my mind.

Poor bastard, dead or disabled, all he was guilty of was wanting us to be dead. Lady Luck was with us again. I was delighted that there were no other cars on the road, because if so we would have had to run to one side of the road or the other and hide in the deep, wet foliage.

But, divine providence or whatever decided we should soon see the headlights of oncoming cars on U.S. 1, and we did. Then I found myself in another quandary - whether to walk north toward Miami or south back towards Key West. If the guys had made a successful connection with their compatriots and were on their way to Big Pine Key, would they be coming up from Key West or down from Miami? I opted for them heading South from Miami – just instinct, I guess. There would be nothing for them in Key West except to possibly find Cody dead. There was always the possibility that he was alive and out there searching for Ruby and me. I opted for that idea too. Tiredness brings its own confusion and I was up to my pretty pink ass in both.

We began to walk South because I knew that Bahia Honda State Park was nearby, somewhere nearby. I wasn't sure if it were North or South of Big Pine Key, but it didn't make any difference because I knew it was close and there would be people camping there. It was still our tourist season, and in spite of the cool, rainy, weather, hardy souls from up North loved to camp out in our tropical wilderness. As we walked, I wracked my tired brain to remember if we had seen a restaurant or hotel nearby. I didn't remember.

The weather was clearing again and although we were wet to the skin and cold, there was only a light tropical breeze to contend with now.

We had been walking and not talking to each other for almost an hour. It was hard walking by the side of the road, especially for Ruby who still had on her white high heels. I was a little more comfortable in my straw espadrilles. But not much. My watch said 9 p.m. and I sort of half remembered that the last time I looked at it, it said a quarter to 8.

And that was way back before the shooting incident. The reason we were not talking was that we just flat out didn't have the energy and there wasn't much to say anyway. Reflect on, yes. Lots to reflect on. How did I ever get myself in this crappy mess?

The cars were whizzing by and I had mixed feelings about trying to get a ride. Probably, many of the cars were driven by locals on their way to another Key. Most of the campers and tourists would be safely in their tents or motels by now. Days are long in the Keys and most visitors have dinner and turn in early to eagerly await another sun and fun filled day. Yeah.

Soon one of the whizzers stopped. Ruby and I looked at the old green Nissan and an older lady with gray hair and smiling blue eyes opened the passenger's side window.

"You gals lost?" she crackled at us.

"Yep, lost, cold and needing a ride to anywhere."

The old Conch-lady - what we natives call someone who was born and raised in the Florida Keys - hit the button to open the door and in an instant, a bedraggled Ruby was in the back seat and I was firmly rooted, wet ass and all in the passenger's seat.

"No telephone?" she quizzed after taking a good look at the state of both of us.

"Seems to me all you youngish folks have those big, gray portable phones, everywhere I go I see 'em."

"Yes ma'am, we have one, but it's back in our car in Key West."

"Key West," she mouthed, wide-eyed, "that's quite a piece down the road." She gave me a good looking-over and said, "especially when you're walkin'. I'm not going that far, but I'll be glad to take you over to Summerland Key."

I smiled a thank you and we rode for a while in silence. Conchs are private people and are known to respect other's privacy as well. So we were in luck. I sure as hell did not feel like trotting out the whole fuckin' drama. She looked kindly enough, with her tanned-like-slightly-burnt-toast smiling face, gray curly hair, denim bib overalls and faded pink shirt. Thank God she kept quiet.

So, what's gonna be the next move? I pondered. A hot bath and a steamy cup of *café Cubano*. Fat chance.

Soon we were at the Key and Mrs. Nichols, our driving angel, pulled up at a Shell station. As in most towns where a major highway runs through, there was a little grocery attached to the gas station. So we went in and saw all the goodies and treats for weary travelers up on wire basket shelves all around the walls. We've all been in places like this, wondering if we should get some pecan-log rolls to munch in the car or take home to the kids. Well, there was no wondering now. Even a Twinky sounded good. I opted for a bag of chips and a Coke as we said our thanks again to Mrs. Nichols, who left us with a smile and some advice.

"No good you two walking any farther in the dark. Ought to get a local taxi and stay in a motel on this Key. See ya," she waved a final goodbye.

I gratefully drank my Coke, feeling the sugar and caffeine race through my energy-starved body, and knew that would put my brain back in high gear. Ruby had the Twinky. The tourists and a couple of the people who worked in the shop and gas station kind of gaped at us. No wonder, the odd sight of two blondes dressed in wet and tattered clothes was not something they saw every day. Ruby's pretty yellow suit was torn in a half dozen places from her trip into the brambles, and my shirt was practically sleeveless from tearing through the woods after her.

189

In view of our obvious dilemma, the clerk said our treats were "on the house." Kind people in the Keys, no doubt about that. The pay phone was just outside and in a moment I phoned home, collect, of course.

Jack sounded worried when he answered the phone.

"Just listen," I said.

"But where?" he asked.

"Just listen," I repeated. "We are at a Shell Station on Summerland Key. We were kidnapped but we're okay. Cody may be dead, last I saw him he was shot and lying on the friggin'' tarmac at …"

"No," Jack interrupted me, "he's all right, had his vest on and-"

I heard little else. Thank you, God, Cody had his problems, but he didn't need to die that way.

Little did I know at that time how predictive that episode was, and how only too soon in our future would more agonizing events visit Cody and once again throw all of our lives into a violent paroxysm of fear and disbelief.

Chapter Twenty-Two

Jack was going on. "Are you listening?" he asked.

"I'll come and get you both. Stay at that gas station – will take me a couple of hours, maybe a little more, but I'll be there."

"Where is Cody?" I ventured.

"He is in Miami, at home. In the morning he will be at the state attorney's office."

I cut in with, "And so will we. That son-of-a-bitch ex-husband of Ruby's tried to have us killed."

"Well, Cody and I have been on the phone constantly," Jack said.

"We were out of our minds with worry. Hassan skipped, we think he's on his way out of the country and ..."

"Where's little Chris? Is he okay? Ruby is out of her mind with worry."

"He's okay, Lita and Cheetah took him up to Lauderdale to a friend's house. He's fine, don't worry. They'd kill the bastard and be glad to do it if he ever came near the kid."

I repeated all of this to a frenzied Ruby, who finally visibly relaxed and kind of slumped up against the telephone booth.

It was just around midnight when Jack arrived. By that time, Ruby and I, a lot drier and a lot more comfortable, had told a few of the locals how we had innocently gotten ourselves into such a predicament. Leaving out all of the important details, we made it seem like a regular kidnapping for money. And they, eyes wide with the excitement and danger of it all and intrigued by our bravery, bought us some tuna sandwiches on rye. We washed them down into our starving little bellies with some hot, black, sweet coffee. American coffee, of course, damn good to me. Keys folks are nice.

Jack was a sight for sore eyes. He looked tired, haggard, had bags under his eyes -worry had taken its toll. He hugged us both and of course had to make a bit of a joke of our predicament, entertainer that he is. But, there was nothing funny about our ordeal, and he knew it.

A short trip down the now less than 30 miles to Key West found us in the courthouse parking lot where my little gold chariot awaited us, alone and lonely.

"Can you drive?" Jack asked me.

"Damn right I can," I said and looked at him like he was nuts. Maybe we were all a little nuts then.

"What choice is there, anyway?"

None. It was about 1 a.m., not even 24 hours since we had set off from Miami, and so much had happened and I had killed someone.

How's that's gonna affect me in time to come? I wondered.

Ruby drove with me and we followed Jack up U.S. 1 back to our safe territory. We had a chance to talk about what had been and what might be coming. I told her why Cody had a Kevlar vest - it did save his life, no doubt about that.

I told her how I asked Cody why he decided to wear the vest on that particular occasion, and his answer surprised me.

"Maybe it's contagious," he said. "Maybe I caught some of that psychic stuff you've always talked about. Don't know. Just had a pesky feeling that this was the day for some serious protection. So I dug it out and put it on. Sure glad I did, Lori."

"I'm sure glad you did too," I told him.

A year or so earlier, we had gone to a gun shop on Okeechobee Road near Hialeah Gardens to pick up some bail bond badges and T-shirts that we had ordered. I kind of jokingly said to Cody, "Say, how about one of these?" as I picked up a silvery, Kevlar vest "One never knows when it might come in handy, does one?" Cody looked at me kind of funny but I could see he was intrigued as he took it from me and handed it to the clerk to add onto the bill. He was always a man of few words.

"Want one, Lori?" he asked.

"Nah, probably don't come in my 'Zip-code', er, I mean size."

We all laughed. As we went out the door I quipped to Cody, "Anyway, I don't get in trouble like you do."

Back on Miami Beach about 4 a.m. I dropped an exhausted exotic-cum-ballet dancer at her door and as she hesitated, I decided to come in with her for a quick sweep. My .38 was in my hand, I was in no mood for any surprises. The apartment was empty and quiet, so with a quick hug and an admonition to lock up really well, I left and drove home.

Before sunrise, I pulled into my driveway and once again realized how lucky I was. To be alive, all in one piece, and living in such a damn nice place. I had called Cody from the car phone on the way up and he sounded very tired but okay. Told him some of the details of the day and night and he said we would meet around 2 p.m. at the state attorney's office.

I had my hot bath and a glass of red wine, deserved it even though it was not my style to drink before breakfast. Ha. Then I slipped into my comfy bed next to my beloved Jack. My hero.

We knew for everyone's sake we had to keep this shit out of the newspapers. It would do none of us any good if the story came out and would really serve no purpose other than to upset a lot of innocent people. The mess in the Keys had been taken care of by some of Cody's unnamed cronies. That's why we have alligators in the Everglades. The State Attorney was bringing all sorts of criminal charges against the now disappeared Hassan and certainly the FBI would have some interest in this matter and be looking for him as well. We- Cody, Ruby, Jack and I- had very little to do. Both kidnappers were dead it seemed, and out of the picture, and all the bad people involved were out of our lives. The caper was over. If Hassan returned to the U.S. he would be detained and arrested. And for sure, that was something that mysterious, enigmatic man did not want to happen.

In the week that followed, Cody told me that he knew about Hassan from sources that preferred to remain anonymous and he admitted to me that he had thought about doing business with him at one time. He thought better of it because he found out from some third parties that Hassan was involved in very nefarious dealings having to do with child pornography and the sex slave trade. Heavy shit. I had many thoughts at different times about Cody being involved with drugs, one way or another. Certainly not using them. But, it was always a murky kind of feeling, fraught with uncertainty. But, I was glad to know that he would never get involved with Hassan and his murderous thugs. I suppose that Cody factored in that working or even knowing Hassan could eventually bring trouble, and Cody was a private, very private man.

Private or not, I still had to find out from him how the hell he happened to turn up in Key West at that fateful moment. He scratched his chin, smiled and said, "I guess you have a right to know after all the crap you went through."

"Yeah, I would say so."

"Well, after I checked out Hassan through some sources in Miami, I got a call from someone I knew in Washington. I'd done some trips with him a few years before and he was concerned about my interest in Hassan. Said he was really bad news, was under surveillance and I should be very careful. When I mentioned your coming trip to Key West, he perked up and told me that Ruby had been watched while she was down there dancing and that an operative was keeping an eye on her. And would do so when you got down there. I asked him if it were a man or a woman and he chuckled and said he was reluctant to say. Later on I found out why. It seems that your guardian-angel was a person named Roberta. Someone you had met when you went down to take Ruby out of jail. Apparently you had been very nice to Roberta, My friend told me he was not certain if she were a she or a he. I really didn't care. I just felt that I should be there and it was a good thing I was. Roberta found me right after the shooting and was able in some way, I'll never know how, to delay communications with the conspirators in Miami who were going to go down and kill you."

Well, that certainly answered a few of my questions.

During the next week I kept in close touch with Ruby. One day she came over to the house in tears. She told me that earlier that day she had received a call from Hassan. He threatened her and said she would have no peace until she gave him their son.

"Lori," she sobbed, "he said he would find me and kill me unless I did what he said."

"My God," I stuttered in shock that Hassan would have such audacity after all that happened. "What did you say?"

Her face became rigid and pale, like a mask worn by a Japanese Samurai as he was about to enter battle.

"I told him," she said and her voice was full of courage and a conviction I'd never heard before, "I told him he would never see me or our son again and I would kill him if he ever came near us."

"Wonderful, Ruby, you are so brave and …"

She interrupted me and continued, "Then I called Roberta on the secret number she gave me and told her what happened. They are coming to my house tonight to make some arrangements. I don't know why, but I think I'll never see you again. Dear Lori, you have been such a good friend to me and Chris. I will never forget you."

And she was right. I never did see her again. Since she had no family in Miami and only a few friends, the FBI decided that in the interest of her safety she and her son, Chris, were to be put in the witness protection program and relocated to a safe spot. Just in case. And so, within the week, Ruby and her beautiful baby boy were gone like the wind. And may God bless them both. Business resumed as usual at Classy Bail Bonds, at least for the time being.

Chapter Twenty-Three

*A*fter finishing that last venture with Miss Ruby, I was delighted to resume my routine of traveling around Florida with Cody to write bonds. It was not dangerous and I'd had my fill of danger for awhile.

We would fly up to Lake Okeechobee or someplace nearby, early in the morning, get our guy out and head back to Miami by midday. Sometimes we would stay up in the middle of the state and have lunch, catfish fried to perfection, or alligator tail. Now, that's a delicacy. Not for everyone, but if you can get past the idea of chewing down on a reptile who is known for his desire to eat a stray dog or small person now and again, and it is properly prepared, it is delicious. As I said, takes some getting used to but I got used to a lot of different things during those days. Eating alligator tail was probably one of the more palatable items on my list.

I never wondered why in the next few months, an increasing number of our cases were drug-based, and why so much of our work was in upstate Florida. Sometimes, when you see a lot of gray, you have to step really far away before you realize that it's an elephant. You just can't tell from up close. And so it went. I was to find out, a few months later, more about the mystery of Cody Williams, and share in a life threatening adventure that I will never forget.

Cody had lots of friends up around Lake Okeechobee and all parts nearby. Cody had lots of friends, period. He spent a good deal of his time in Central Florida and was buying a large parcel of land near the lake, about two hundred acres. I asked how he could put together such a big chunk of money, for even though we did all right, a million-dollar piece of land could take quite a bite out of anyone's bankroll. Unless, of course, that bankroll was unlimited, and funded by laundered cash from a nearby coastal state like Louisiana, Alabama or possibly the Carolinas. It took me about a year to figure that one out. But, just about every day it was business as usual at Classy Bail Bonds. Cody chose that name. Cody loved the business, and assured me in his usual casual way, that there was going to be plenty of money coming in, that our earnings were on the increase, and that he was being partially financed by a group of investors who had taken an interest in us.

If I were really on the alert, I'd have seen that pretty scarlet red flag waving. But I didn't. Cody was a brilliant manipulator in a very fortuitous, unconcerned manner. He easily kept me from getting too concerned about the situation by telling me that he was planning, after the purchase, to sell off a small, perhaps 20 acre tract to Jack and me. He knew we were anxious to buy some land to hold for our retirement and explained that the new area would be perfect for us.

In the coming year, shortly after the land purchase was completed, Cody started work on a large landing strip right in the middle of the property. He spent weekends up there supervising the project and living in a large mobile home that had been purchased for just that purpose. None of the financial aspects that in any way concerned the purchase of the land, the strip or the mobile home had anything to do with me. A separate account was set up between Cody and some other people whom I did not know. It was really none of my business, had nothing to do with Classy Bail Bonds, Inc., and anyway, pretty soon Jack and I would get our 20 acres. I contented myself, at least for the time being, with the knowledge of that.

One day Cody said to me, "Well, Honey," (his Southern name for me) "Looks like you and Jack are gonna become property owners one day in the near future. I just have to get some stuff worked out and then the southwest twenty is yours. Probably take a year or two, but be patient," he smiled, "it's a done deal."

Thrilled wasn't the word for it.

As time went on and I saw the tremendous amount of money being put into the land, I did begin to wonder who the hell was putting up the cash and why. But it was all under Cody's name. I kept reminding myself that I really had nothing to do with the whole deal. I was only his partner in Classy Bail Bonds, Inc. And all our bonds were written for a very responsible law firm with a sterling reputation. They were an impeccable group of young lawyers who would never dream of doing anything that even smacked of being tainted or outside the law. The bonds were all collateralized and the law firm stood behind each and every one of their clients. Safe enough for me, I reasoned.

Finally Jack and I had some loose cash to buy property we had been aching to have for some time. So, once and for all, I quit worrying about all the whys and wherefores.

Then one day, about six months later, Cody came in to the office and told me he was going to be away for a few days.

He said to me, "I'm flying someone down to Colombia on a private charter, a sweet little stretch 727. We're going to pick up some equipment, and I'm taking Victor with me for company. We will come back after the weekend."

From time to time, Cody took off by himself for a kind of secret mission, and I never asked any questions about it. I could run the office by myself and there were no bonds that needed writing immediately. So I was not alarmed or concerned. I should have been a bit more aware, but hindsight is almost always 20/20. Actually, I was glad that our attorney friend Victor was going with him and I knew the trip would turn into a bit of a fun breakaway for them both. Victor had a penchant for making things fun and I could see why Cody had chosen him to go along.

That short interval turned into nearly five months. Cody, his friend and attorney, Victor, and I could easily have lost our lives, and when the ordeal finally ended, we took a vow of silence for many, many reasons. Cody, Victor and I shared a strange and very secret adventure, and that secret burned in our hearts and some would say really changed our lives forever.

After the return from Colombia, it became business as usual for all of us and it was only when we crept into the deep recesses of our memories that the fears reminiscent of what had transpired and what a terrible ending could have befallen us came back to haunt us.

Chapter Twenty-four

It began when Cody, who was an excellent pilot with a great reputation, was recruited by some people in Miami to fly an empty stretch 727 down to Colombia and return the following day with a load of farming supplies.

This was a year or so after we opened our business and things were going along very smoothly. Apparently Cody was preparing to take the final state exam and get licensed. It seemed that in the interest of making some big bucks, Cody decided to put everything on hold and go down to Colombia. But, there was more to it than a simple flight, as I was soon to find out. Cody asked Victor to accompany him. He promised him a great time in Colombia for a few days, and then the trip back.

When I found out about the planned trip to Colombia I had trepidations. Even before Colombia, I felt he was on a pathway of disaster.

In my way, I cared a lot for Cody. How could I not? He was generous, very kind to me and caring in a sort of guarded way that I came to understand and accept. And I saw his potential! I agonized over my feelings that he was quietly hurtling down a path toward disaster. Nevertheless, when I had the opportunity to join them, I did.

"Sounds good to me," Victor said when he told me I was going along.

I was not there for the first part of the journey but Victor told me the whole story. Believe me, he left nothing out. He began at the very beginning, flying out of Miami on the big airplane. Victor explained to me that Cody had a friend, Roger, who would serve as his copilot.

Victor said, "I know nothing about flying airplanes. I was just along for the ride, and it was an eerie, spooky feeling being all alone, just the three of us, me, Cody and Roger, on that gigantic airplane."

At the time Victor told me, I could almost feel the nervous tension on that airplane.

Victor said it was so noisy he could hardly think. The whirring of the engines was driving him crazy and Cody and Roger were so busy flying the goddamn plane that they had no time to talk to him. He walked back into the main cabin a couple of times, but it was really creepy with no one in the few seats that were left. Most of the seats had been removed so we could carry the equipment back.

It was easy for me to feel what he was going through, for Victor had an expressive manner, and he left little to the imagination once he got started. Trouble was, half of what he said was in Spanish and the rest in unintelligible English but even so, I was able to understand much of what he said for I had learned to speak Spanish long ago. Then he stopped cold and began to cry. He cried very bitterly for some time and then continued with his story.

He said there was a lot of *turbulencio*, turbulence, the sky seemed to be going crazy all around them, it was a very dark gray and then black as coal. The wind and rain were tossing them around like an umbrella in a hurricane, and the engines were very loud. Cody was having a hard time handling the airplane, it seemed that they were rising and falling so much. He asked Cody why it was happening and he said he had to keep going higher to avoid the storm and then drop down to his normal flight altitude.

If ever there were a man born to be a pilot, it was Cody. He and the airplane were as one most of the time, and after a couple of hours, the rain and wind stopped and they sort of settled into the adventure of it all.

They traveled with Roger. He rarely spoke. In fact, Victor said, there were times when they had flown together and he always kind of ignored him, so he was accustomed to his behavior and more or less accepted it. Actually, he tried very hard to fall asleep on the floor of the cockpit, behind the two of them, but he could not, even though he was exhausted, and so it was not much of a rest. The floor was covered with an old carpet, gray, dirty and torn in many places. Victor did not want to put his face down but, as tired as he was, eventually found himself with the hard, sandpaper-like rug up against his cheek. Victor's eyes were smarting from tears as the fetid mildew smell plagued his lungs. Sleep still evaded him and he lay there staring up at nothing but silver colored rounded walls ending in a curved ceiling overhead.

After what seemed like forever but was actually only about four or five hours, Cody told them to prepare for landing. Victor didn't know what he expected him to do. There were no tray tables to put up and his seat back was in the proper position, so, with his seat belt on, Victor called out that he was ready. Cody gave him a strange look and proceeded to land the airplane.

Funny thing about Cody, he loved airplanes like he loved women, and he could never bear to insult either. He felt it was insulting to call an airplane a plane, and he never did so. It was always, "I'm going up in my airplane," or "My airplane needs servicing."

Weeks before this incident, I felt that I was beginning to get some insight into Cody's character. I really appreciated his easygoing, devil-may-care attitude, though I knew that deep inside of him there was an agitated and somewhat untamed energy that few ever got to see. He was polite and apparently self effacing, but I was beginning to realize that was just part of the façade he showed to the world.

Victor told me that as soon as the airplane was on the ground, Cody told him to help Roger open the doors and said that he should keep out of the way as some men would be loading the farm equipment and they would be leaving as soon as that was done.

Cody always had a "let's get there and be done with it" attitude, which, coupled with his fortitude, usually left lesser humans worn out.

Then everything changed. It all happened so damn fast, Victor later told me. The doors were opened, two of them, one front and one aft. Then two Colombian guys came aboard.

Victor spoke to them and they asked who was the "*Jefe*," the chief.

Victor pointed at Cody and in a quick move one of the men grabbed Cody's right hand, pumping it for all he was worth, smiled a gold-toothed smile and immediately stepped to the forward door and waved to two more men who were standing just outside the airplane. Victor thought it was strange that no customs men were there to greet them in that early morning dawn. The whole damn thing was strange, played out in that ethereal light with three of the men chattering away in Spanish and Cody silent, just standing with his arms crossed over his chest.

Victor asked Cody if they could get off the airplane for a few minutes, so he could regain his composure, and he said "okay," but stayed near the airplane. He walked down the little gangplank that had been set up at the aft door and felt the cool fresh air of an early Colombian morning. It washed over him like a Spring rain and he was instantly refreshed. The beauty of the nearby wooded area was breathtaking, disappearing into majestic mountains and clear cloudless skies.

Victor said that he could see towering mountains all around them so he guessed that they must be high up in the Andes, somewhere in the middle of Colombia. Colombia is a dangerous place. It is a country long known to us as a place where they grow cocaine and smuggle it into the States. Period. It is also the area with the largest rain forest in the world and has the Amazon River running through it. But other than that, Victor had no idea where the hell they were. He finally asked a most distracted Cody, and he said they were in the Andes, in a place called Popayan, and the nearest big city was Cali. At least that made him aware of where they were, but he thought everyone knew about the Cali cartel, and what the hell were they getting into?

Cody came down the gangplank a minute after Victor did, with Roger right behind him.

"Hey, Poncho," a very agitated Roger said to him.

Victor thought it was bad enough the rude little creep ignored him most of the time, but to call him by any name other than Victor was unthinkable. He was annoyed. Roger then told him to ask if the Colombians had any coffee, any café, and then added that he really needed a cup of java to get going.

He asked one of the men who was busy loading equipment onto the airplane and he answered, "*Esta usted loco? No hay café aqui*," and he laughed.

About a half hour later, with the sun coming up and the temperature rising a bit as a complement to the beautiful sunrise, two more workers appeared and they brought with them some small, heavy equipment. The stuff looked like small plows and heavy wheelbarrows covered with a gray, dirty looking canvas.

Victor wondered why on earth it would be necessary to bring that farming stuff to the States. Surely it could be bought at any local hardware store in the U.S.A.., even better stuff, and new as well. He was nobody's fool, a superb attorney later to become a foremost jurist and erstwhile public official. He was just about to ask this of Cody when he heard loud voices coming from the woods.

"*Mira, mira!*" they said.

And in an instant a half dozen Colombian p*olicia*, police, came out of the wooded area with guns and what looked like bayonets. They charged up to the airplane and as Roger made a very quick move to get back on the airplane, he was caught in a cross-fire of bullets coming in their direction. Cody told Victor to stand still and be quiet. He didn't have to say much, he was terrified. Seeing Roger shot down that way gave Victor a real severe reality adjustment. Was he next? And what about Cody? After all, he was the '*Jefe.*' Those questions remained unanswered for the moment as a half dozen p*olicia* boarded the airplane and began rapidly removing our newly installed 'cargo' and cautioning them to stay put.

What the hell was that all about? he thought, but the truth was he really knew the answer before he asked the question. It was becoming more and more obvious. Drugs.

The police stepped over Roger's dead body and never even looked at Cody or him for a long while. Then one of the p*olicia*, I guess he was the captain, told one of the others to go and get *el carro*. Even Cody understood that much Spanish. In a minute a green, battered old military jeep arrived on the scene and they were ordered to get into it. Cody cautioned Victor silently, by a look, to keep his mouth shut. He didn't have to worry.

A long drive through the mountains on a really badly broken-up road took us to a clearing and from there onto a paved road to what looked like a small village. I suppose it had a name, but it was quite a while before they got to know it. Santa Agostina, a name that inspires the furies of hell to ravage through my debilitated spirit, even to this very day.

They were treated fairly well, no rough stuff, but since they had not uttered a word and they did not know Victor spoke Spanish, they talked about the two remaining *gringos* in a very insulting manner. Victor thought, who cared? because they were still alive, although obviously in custody of some sort. He wondered what they had done but the gnawing feeling in his gut told him that Cody had really gotten them into deep shit this time. Whether he

211

knew or not didn't really matter at this point. But without a doubt, they were in it, up to their necks.

Then it finally dawned on his innocent, but somewhat idiotic self, how could he have been so foolish as not to know that they were going there with only one purpose in mind, to bring back a load of drugs from Colombia? It seemed like everyone else knew. What a rush that was. He ran the gamut of mixed emotions. How could Cody put him at risk like this? This was the man they trusted.

It became very brutal, they started to ask Cody lots of questions in broken English, Spanglish was more like it. He never broke a sweat, but tried to answer them as honestly as he could. No, he did not know drugs were being loaded onto his airplane. No, he did not know the whole name of the man in Miami Beach who had approached him for this job. He only knew him as Carlosito. He had been introduced by someone, another pilot, an American, over at the Opa Locka Airport where he kept his other airplanes. No, this was not his airplane, it was on loan for a few days, only to do this job, and must be returned by the weekend.

Victor only suspected then, that the airplane would never be returned to American soil and that they didn't believe a word he said. And what's more, he realized at that point it would be only by the grace of God, and Cody's wherewithall and ability to look ahead, that they would remain alive and ever see Miami again.

Chapter Twenty-Five

They found out soon enough that Victor spoke Spanish and their attempts to communicate with him, although he answered their questions as honestly as he could, left them frustrated and annoyed.

Not content with the answers they got from Cody, and agitated by Victor's obvious lack of knowledge about what was going on, the two seeming top guns ordered their men to put Cody and Victor in a holding cell. It had a bare wooden floor, full of splinters, and a roof made of tar paper covered over with wood. It was very strong and had bars on all four sides. Actually, he felt that it was more like a cage, a very strong wooden cage with bars made of steel, standing just outside the building where they had been interrogated. It was probably built to house just two medium-size people, and then only if they didn't stand up. Cody was over 6 feet tall, and Victor, although not exactly a peanut, wondered how the hell would they both fit in?

They fit in there all right, and it was close, but eventually they got used to it. What choice did they have? They had a large gray tarpaulin-like rag that dropped down over the front bars at night and, let me tell you, it really stank. The upside was that it kept the rain from coming in. The cell was pushed up against the building and so they had protection from there as well, but the two sides were open to the wind and sun, as well as the rain, and it got very uncomfortable.

I suppose they thought that if Victor and Cody got miserable enough, they would give them more information. But Victor had nothing to tell, except what an asshole he was for being sucked into this ridiculous position, and if Cody knew any more, he wasn't talking.

The food, if you can call it that, was really disgusting. Every morning around breakfast time and then again in the early evening they were served a small wooden bowl filled with a mix of beans, re-fried, many times, swimming in a jelly like foul fish smelling liquid with an occasional slice of *bacalao*, a type of dried codfish on top. Twice a day this marvelous concoction was served to them. At dinnertime it was almost bearable, but they loathed having it for breakfast. Once in awhile at mid-day they would get a banana, and how they savored that seemingly rare and delicious fruit. And that was only due to Cody's influence over their food distributor.

He was another story, a young man of about 18, lame, tall and thin and obviously mentally retarded. He smelled like his clothing had not been changed in a year, but to them he appeared like an angel of mercy. He had a very practical side to him as well, and he handled the uncomfortable task of taking care of their sanitation, which, believe me, was no simple chore since they were not permitted to go outside their little cage. He was thoughtful and kind to them and handled his backbreaking drudgery in a very matter of fact manner. And, for all his seeming lack of sophistication, he was staunch, and after a very short time it became obvious that he, Cody and Victor had very few secrets from each other.

One day about a week after they arrived, aware of their obvious discomfort in having a splintered wooden floor, he brought them an old piece of worn and yellowed carpet to stand on. It was an act of kindness that they truly appreciated. When he smiled, he exposed badly rotted teeth in a face pathetically covered by pimples that had more or less come together to give him a permanent red rash look. No beauty this Ramon. But he was their man, and as kind to them as anyone ever was during that entire horrible adventure.

The time they spent with him, cooped up as they were, was probably no less than two months. He wondered many times how they would survive.

The filth, the degradation, the acrimony. They were like pigs given slop for their meals which they eventually came to wait in hope for. What else was there to do? At least once a day, a man or woman

215

came over dressed in army-type fatigues and asked them if they had anything to tell them. They virtually ignored Cody, referring to him as the "gringo pig".

The woman guard was very nice to Victor and once even offered him a cigarette. She was not offended when he refused the cigarette, shrugged and went on to tell him that if they could talk to the "*jefe*" things would go easier for them when they finally went to trial before the *tribunal de justicia*. She clammed up momentarily when Victor asked her when that might happen, and finally said that sometimes they kept prisoners in this form of isolation for six months, especially when drugs were involved.

"You see," the woman guard went on in perfect Spanish, softly, as if for his ears only, "things are very sensitive right now. There is a very big alliance happening between a lot of factions of the coca industry. And it is an industry now, your being here proves that."

She went on, "The alliance or unification is happening between the narcotic traffickers and some guerilla groups making the sale of the coca into a real business, and I am predicting that this is just the beginning. So many of the *campesinos* and farmers are turning to coca and giving up growing the traditional crops.

"*Si, muchos problems vienen aqui,*" she said. "There are many problems coming here."

And how right she was, for that was truly just the beginning.

She was really quite pleasant, had her job to do, of course, that is, to try to get as much out of them as she could, but her tactic was a real soft sell. On the other hand, Fernando, the male guard, was a real commando type. He screamed at them in Spanish and spat at Cody every chance he got.

Actually, it was almost comical, these two people who were told to interrogate them day after day. It was like the old good guy, bad guy game that everyone knows how to play. Only it was no game. Fernando would come to see them at odd hours. Sometimes they would open their eyes at the break of dawn to see this fat *bandillero* sitting there staring at them, sweating, his foul breath polluting the little fresh air that managed to get through to them. Who knows how long he'd been there, but his comment was always the same.

"Eh, Chico, you want to tell me why you come to Colombia?" he would say. "You want to tell me who paid you *dinero* to come here with the big airplane?"

And Victor's response, for Cody would never speak to him, was always, "*Jefe, no hay nada que decir.*" Or in other words, I have nothing to say.

This always infuriated him, but nonetheless he remained for 10 minutes or so, harassing Victor, in particular, because he knew the language, but making terrible references to his "fancy man." Nothing could have been further from the truth. We always believed Cody was straight as an arrow and God help the man who approached him otherwise. But this greasy, fat bastard was in there pitching all the time. They knew what he wanted, and he for one could tell him nothing. And Cody wasn't talking. Time had no meaning for them.

There was no doubt that they would have rotted in that jail cell. Something had to be done. Someone had to rescue them and that's where I came into the picture.

Chapter Twenty-Six

My cousin Carol is married to a wonderful man who originally came from Colombia. Jose has been in Miami many years and they have a good marriage and three great kids. The rest of his family is still back in Medellin, which is one of the nicest parts of Colombia. They have money, and a business and live a good life. From time to time, Carol and Jose go over to see his father and mother who are in their 70s now.

Truth is indeed stranger than fiction, because that is exactly how I was able to find Cody and Victor. Carol and Jose were in Medellin for a summer vacation, and were to return in about six weeks. Actually, Carol was a bit concerned for her in-laws and both she and her darling Jose were trying to persuade them to come to live in Miami, for a lot of reasons, safety being the most obvious. They had a big house, the kids were getting older, soon to go to college, and there was plenty of room for the older couple and certainly enough love to go around.

It came to pass that in a very off-handed manner Jose's dad mentioned to him that a few weeks before there had been an article in the newspaper about some Americans. Apparently two of them, both men, were being held after their arrest for some possible involvement with cocaine smuggling. The article showed a photograph of two tall, bearded men, one with light hair, the other dark, almost Latin-looking.

Jose's father, Domingo, took an interest because his son was living in the States and he thought that they mentioned the men were from Florida. But he never mentioned it until Carol and came to see them. While they were back in Miami, a few weeks prior to their visit to Colombia, I told Carol that Cody had more or less disappeared and for some reason I thought he was in South America.

I eventually did go to Colombia and of course it was on an airplane, and yes, I was fuckin' scared out of my wits. But a lot happened before I went. First of all Carol, by some kind of magic, was able to get hold of the newspaper article and recognized Cody even though he looked quite different. I had to be really careful as well, because they are very distrustful down there and because of her in-laws I could not afford to arouse any suspicion that could come back to hurt them. The big cities are well-populated and very cosmopolitan, but where the guys were, is simply rural, rugged and unsophisticated and terribly dangerous. Santa Agostina, in the middle of fuckin' nowhere.

I didn't think, I just knew that he was my partner and I would have to go. Who else would or could go? Brad and Sam were busy as hell and not too crazy about Cody in the first place, and in the second place, I was very low-key. I could and did bring money into the country, lots of money so that I could literally buy their way out of Colombia. I thought it would be easy. I carried $100 bills in a cloth body stocking tied around my waist. I may have looked a little strange and bumpy around the waistline, especially to me, but no one suspected me. Looked a little plump in the middle, but then who the hell was really looking? I registered with Immigration, informing them that I had family nearby and a more or less safe place to stay. It should have been a breeze, but turned out quite different.

First, I had to get some money. Jack gave me a couple thousand and I wrote a check on our bail bonds account for $3000 more. I could not tell anyone, which would have brought publicity and God only knows what else down on our heads. That was the last thing we wanted. The next problem, after I had the money and a ticket to Medellin, was to let Cody know I was there and had money to pay what most assuredly would be a ransom of sorts. Even that turned into a nightmare when we discovered from some of Jose's sources that a lot of important people were really pissed at Cody. Something about money being paid up front and never seen again. Fuck me, I sure as hell never saw any of it. As I said before, Cody played his cards and his cash close to his chest at the best of times, so what else could we expect?

I was in a real quandary. Jack felt that I could do it because no one would suspect me, and he knew I was a tough little cookie. We didn't even tell Cody's wife, Elaine, because she reacted funny a lot of the time and we couldn't afford to have her blow it for me.

Cody was married to Elena. A marriage essentially born in hell. A cruel joke of sorts, an ice queen married to a quietly hot, seething volcano. These were tumultuous times Elena came from a wealthy Southern Baptist family. Religious as hell, but she had no happy music in her soul. The melody that sometimes appeared was gray and dismal. Cody was the quintessential player of tunes. I observed her on many occasions, saw through to her distant behavior, her abstract involvement in all things family or business and her truly chilly, unapproachable demeanor. But still in all I usually don't like to make judgments about people's personal lives, since I don't like them making judgments about me. Or my friends and family. God knows, we may be sinners all, so be it.

I had always recognized from looking deeply into and beyond his eyes that Cody was troubled. You could tell that he was tormented, it was an always thing with him, didn't come and go. Although at that time, before I went to Colombia, I knew nothing about any relationship that he might be having, never even thought about it, I soon realized when I did find out that perhaps he ultimately found the warmth he so desperately sought in the arms of Mirabella, even if it was only for a little while. Actually, I had never seen him show any love toward anyone, except perhaps his daughter, so it was good that Victor told me that Cody was intensely passionate about this girl.

So I boarded an airplane and landed six hours later in Medellin. It was late afternoon when we arrived. I said we, but it was really just me and an airplane full of, for the most part, Colombian passengers. They seemed to be a sullen lot, certainly not like the holiday fun-goers that flew out of the dear old U.S. of A. into some romantic Caribbean islands, all set for some extravagant and fabulous revelry, whoop-de-doo and merry-making in the fun and sun capitals of the world.

No, this was different. I felt their seriousness like a fabric made up of layers of spider web-like cloth spread over them, with only their grim and somber brown eyes visible above the wrappings that seemed to enfold them.

The uneventful trip ended with the big Avianca Boeing 737 jet being skillfully maneuvered between the two majestic mountain peaks that herald the skyway entrance to the lovely city of Medellin. It seemed to me to be touch and go, but to all the others it appeared to be a very routine approach. The mountains looming in the background gave a shadowy effect in the almost eerie darkness of the evening and added to my feeling that there was a definite gloominess awaiting me.

No, indeed, this was not the lush, luxuriant Colombian countryside that I had imagined as we flew over the green jungle hillsides and verdant, densely forested landscape a few hundred miles before. But, no matter what, I was here and what the hell, that was all I really cared about anyway.

Arrangements had been made for me to take a taxi from the Jose Maria Cordova Airport into Medellin. After clearing Immigration and informing them with my sweet little American voice and a smile to match, that I was visiting their fair city to partake of some of their wonderful cultural events, I moved on to the customs area.

The mustachioed, darkly handsome young customs agent smiled appreciatively as I handed him the customs form, which he scarcely glanced at. I kind of giggled that I was an aficionado of Fernando Botero, their magnificent artiste extraordinare who specialized in glamorizing and indeed romanticizing the lovely rotund, overweight women that were his idea of the magnificent women of Colombia. The customs officer looked lustfully at my luxurious blond hair, my voluptuous bosom and slim figure, and once again smiled his admiration. His gaze was so exacting and his smile so engaging, I almost had the feeling he was undressing me with his eyes. Actually, that was not too unusual. Lots of men did the same thing, some with a bit more flair, however. It was kind of flattering in a more or less kinky way.

He never noticed my little financial bulge, and of course never even suspected the true reason for my visit to his cultural climate.

I have taken taxis before in foreign lands, from foreign airports and sometimes under situations of severe duress. But, I have never felt so glad to get away from any airport as I was that night. It was as if a million shaded, dark brown eyes were searing into my consciousness, asking for a truth that I could not reveal. And it was presumably a lot more than just that. I was probably a little scared. After all, I am pretty human most of the time and this was the beginning of a really scary operation. I'd been downplaying it, but now the truth was I was scared out of my wits. It felt better to finally admit that to myself and then I was able to give myself a little mental shake and really move into the whole goddamn thing. After the usual negotiations, the taxi took off and I was under way to the hotel where I was to meet my confederates. I breathed a sigh of relief. First part done. Lots more to come.

The ride from the airfield was absolutely delightful. Once away from the airport, we were driving on a beautiful new highway, apparently just finished within the past few months. A black and shiny asphalt road. The newly set roadbed glistened like little diamonds underneath the wheels of the rickety taxi as it made its way through soft, rolling countryside. The towering mountains rose like shadowy giants fabricating a mystical backdrop to this new, exciting and terrifying adventure.

Chapter Twenty-Seven

*O*f course, I didn't know what was happening to Cody and Victor at the time of my ride into Medellin, didn't even know for sure if they were still alive or where the hell they were. Soon after I met up with them, Victor filled me in on all the details and this is the continuation of what he told me of his daily life in the cage. I could hear his voice.

He said, "After what must have been about eight weeks of total neglect, a little sunshine came into our blistered lives, very little sunshine," Victor said. "It was in the form of a young girl whom we assumed was brought to gape at us in our cage by our retarded but kindly jailer, Ramon."

"*Mira. Mira,*" Ramon said to her as she timidly approached the cage of these two Americanos with beards and long filthy hair.

Her name was Maribella, meaning pretty sea or ocean, and she was pretty in a strange kind of way.

Her eyes were a rich sea green and her skin was deeply tanned. Actually, she could have been a real beauty if her perfection not been marred by a searing white scar that went from just under her left eye down her cheek then curved all the way to the top of her upper lip.

What tragedy caused that, Victor wondered, but content with her pretty smile, and busy wallowing in his own disgust, he decided not to wonder too much. Strangely enough, *she* looked with pity on Cody and Victor, and Victor could see that she had a tender heart, probably born of years of being stared at and worse. It occurred to him how unexpected it is where and when compassion shows itself. After a few minutes of conversation now and then, over the weeks of our imprisonment, Ramon knew that Victor was some sort of compatriot. At least they had a language in common, and not just the commonality of their respective filth.

About two days after Maribella's visit, late one night, a man came out of the shadows and approached the cage. Victor could hardly contain his excitement. Who was he? What did he want, and was he another of their tormenters?

The man who came that night was Maribella's uncle. He came because she had told him about them. and their plight. He came because he was a greedy bastard who figured he could make a lot of *pesos* out of their degradation and misery. But he looked like a saint to them.

He told them he could get them out of there if they were willing and able to pay. Also, that he could

227

help them along in their escape to Cali, about 100 miles away. He would help them get from where they were through to the northern regions of Colombia and into Venezuela, then escape back to the United States.

A cold fear gripped Victor. What were they supposed to do for money? It's not like they could wire home via Western Union. Hopeless, again.

Cody spoke to Victor in a hushed tone, "Don't worry about the money. Ask him how much he wants. No, better yet, tell him I have a hundred American dollars to give him if he can get us out of here and on our way."

A hundred dollars? Where the hell did that come from? Victor wondered.

But, he said what Cody told him to say even though he said he kept thinking, where the hell could he have a stash? Even if Cody did not appear to be, Victor was concerned about the money. Again, Cody told him not to worry, just talk fast. So he did. The old bastard had probably never seen 100 American dollars, and had little chance of ever hoping to. So his guard dropped a bit and he stammered out a *'si, si'* in agreement.

Victor hissed to Cody, and he said, "Okay, now whatcha gonna do?"

He said, "Tell him to come back late tomorrow night, alone, and we will do a deal."

He translated this into Spanish and the old man immediately took off in the direction of the wooded area.

Cody was very tired and told Victor not to ask any more questions of him that night. He said he had a lot of figuring out to do. So, leaning on each other, as they always had to do in order to rest comfortably, they fell into a troubled sleep.

The following day felt like it was a week long, hot, dusty, and the sky though threatening rain did not open up even though the humidity had to be nearing the 100 percent mark. They waited and waited. Ramon brought them their meals and with a wink told them he knew about last night's meeting. Finally it got to be dusk and then an uneasy darkness set in. There was no wind at all, and they could hardly breathe, that's how close and humid it was.

Cody told Victor he had the $100 for the old man. He played his cards very close to his vest, as usual, but, he did tell Victor that the money he had, about $2000, was in the heels of his very worn and shabby boots.

Clever guy, he even thought to wear a pair of old looking boots so that in case of any incident they would not look as if they could be of any value to anyone. So, their lives hung in the balance as to whether or not one of these Latino clowns had wanted Cody's friggin' boots as a souvenir or God knows what else. Believe me, after all they'd been through, the boots really looked like *mierda* or shit.

He apparently had removed a hundred-dollar bill sometime during the night. Victor didn't know it since he was so fast asleep. But Cody is a slick guy.

229

They waited all through that blistering, dusty day, and it was awful. They were both nerved up and it seemed Victor's patience had come to the breaking point, like he was going over the edge with apprehension and anxiety. And then as the hot, fiery sun slipped back down over the dusky mountain, they heard a sound. A low, soft, whistly sound that reverberated through the nearby bushes and trees. Cody and Victor looked at each other in the dimming light and fear washed over Victor like a cascading waterfall. Of course, Cody was as nonplussed as ever, or at least he acted that way. Then it was quiet again. The anticipation was making Victor crazy. More minutes passed, seemed like hours and probably was, for it seemed to be very late when the old man came to them and whispered that he was waiting until all the *gentes*, or, people around the building had gone. Apparently, this was a Saturday night. They actually never really knew what day or night it was, nor did it make any difference to them. Somehow, Saturday night held a real significance for their jailers, who usually had a wild evening and the next morning came in looking a bit partied out. In retrospect, the next day Victor and Cody were able to figure out that the night before was indeed Saturday. Strange, the machinations that their overwrought minds were creating. But, it must have been a Saturday because the buzz came to them that everyone was going to a fiesta in another part of town, making this the perfect night to escape.

It sounded good although Victor had lots of reservations, about the old man, about everything.

But Cody was cool as usual and told him to relax and just go with the flow.

He would have literally given anything he owned or ever would own to get out of that hell hole.

The old man had a rather unique way of getting them out. Victor wondered how he would do it, but it didn't take long for them to find out. He first lifted the filthy tarpaulin and threw it to the ground and then using a very large crowbar, actually pried off the top of the cage. He told them to stand up and push as he stood on a large box made of wood, and lifted and pushed the boards off the top onto the ground. The heavy stuff gone, all that was on top of them was some partially melted tar-paper, which they easily pushed up and over the sides.

And they stood up. They stood up for the first time in what seemed to them to have been forever. They both easily climbed out of the now roofless cage onto the ground. The air was sweet, sweeter than it had ever been, and Victor's hungry nostrils inhaled until he thought his lungs would burst. Amazing! Even though there were bars on two sides, and sometimes the tarpaulin was lifted, they never got any of the clean, fresh air that flowed around them, seemingly in torrents, but in actuality, in just little ripples of wind. It was still as hot as hell, and disagreeably damp, but it felt like paradise to them.

The old man told them to hurry and since they were traveling light, to take nothing with them. They moved very quickly. They got out of the area of the cage and away from the building that had loomed darkly behind them for so long, and moved into the shadows leading to the wooded area. The old man, Tio, asked Cody for the *dinero*. Cody gave him the rolled up $100 bill and they were off without another word. The old man was sure footed and kept them on a semi-path in the very dark and gloomy thicket. Hearing all the wildlife sounds sort of unnerved him, but Cody assured him again that the old man knew what he was doing. Out here in the jungle, woods, whatever the hell they were, animals were on the loose. Their fervent cries echoed all around them and reminded him of what his grandfather once said to me when we were out camping in the Everglades together. He was just a kid and scared shitless by the whooping cries of the birds that seemed to be circling overhead. The noise was unbelievably loud and fierce and Victor was certain they were about to meet their doom. But *Abuelo* just went about the business of setting up their tent and smiling at him. He said very little except that they were in their territory and they were as surprised to see them as they were to hear them. He calmed down and smiled at his loving dear old *Abuelo,* and never forgot what he said.

Reason returned, fear evaporated, but Christ, at least they were out.

After being cramped in such a confined space for so long, it was not as easy to move as it could have been. Tio took this into account and was really very considerate of them, although he cautioned about the need to get far away as soon as possible. They trod on for about two or three hours - the woods were thick and very nearly impenetrable in spots -

and from time to time they had to cross little muddy streams, which served to cool them off a bit.

The mosquitoes were enormous and ravenous as well. Not too much gringo blood passes their way and apparently they wanted to make the most of this delicious tidbit of flesh, But, Tio, having knowledge of the area, had foreseen this and had given both Cody and Victor heavy, long sleeved cotton shirts to wear. They sure smelled better than what they had been wearing since their departure from Miami months before, which by now was soaked in sweat and filth.

Deep into the wooded and hilly area, and many hours away from their former place of captivity, Tio stopped and pointed to a small cabin. He told them they would rest there.

They were exhausted, but by no means were they ready for the surprise that awaited them inside the cabin. For there, looking nearly as exhausted as they, were Ramon and Maribella.

What the hell were they doing here? Victor questioned, but Cody told him to slow down and wait a minute, that it would all come crystal clear very soon. It sure did. Apparently, Tio wanted them to take Maribella along with them, he wanted her to be brought safely to Medellin where she might have what he called a "new face" operation, and give her a chance for a life. So the old bastard really did have a heart, and also an ulterior motive for setting them free. He also had $100 to pay a plastic surgeon, assuming they took her and arrived in one piece.

233

It was almost more than Victor could absorb and he really felt like just crying, from exhaustion, from fear of what they were getting into, from the sheer exhilaration of the escape, and from who knows what else. Looking around he saw several cots with cotton blankets thrown across them, and he knew that if they all took a rest, they'd feel better about things when they awoke more refreshed. He guessed they were all thinking the same thing. As he was falling asleep, Victor's last waking thought was that this was Cody's party, so it was up to him to decide who went and who stayed.

When they were all slowly waking up, blazing sunshine punctured the only small window frame that had no glass in it, and served to brighten the tiny cabin they were in. Tio was up and about in a flash and brewed some strong something from the pack he had been carrying. Coffee, more or less, strong and pungent and hot. It gave each of them the jolt that they needed to pull themselves together. Bitter, no sugar or cream, but it tasted good to him. Their conversation of last evening continued, with Victor translating the old man's pleas and Ramon's reasons to Cody, who looked as complacent as ever.

Who would have ever thought it could happen to them? Here they were at the ass end of some friggin' mountainous region, hot, tired, and tormented. Surrounded by Spanish speaking, poverty stricken strangers trying to convince them to further encumber themselves in this mosquito ridden forest. They wanted them to bring this pathetic girl to her salvation in Medellin, many, many miles away, over mountainous territory that they would be crossing on foot while hopefully escaping the forces determined to bring them back to their *justicia*.

Who the fuck did they think they were, the A Team?

Chapter Twenty-Eight

That was the downside of the entire situation.

But, they were soon told what the benefits would be. The upside was that Maribella knew the way. Furthermore, she had family and friends along the way who would feed and shelter them enroute and help them travel the dangerous area through which they had to pass. And she would be able to send messages ahead so that the rest of our journey would be made a lot easier and most certainly safer.

Most of the woods were behind them, but they still had to pass through hilly, rocky dangerous areas, where some of the time they would be exposed, not only to the elements, but to the *policia* and who knows what else. So Maribella acted as sort of a travel guide.

Victor knew it could be worse.

Just before they all left the cabin, Tio looked Cody straight in the eye and said, "*Señor,* you must have really pissed off some *importante gentes*, because there is much talk around the camps that some of the guerrillas and traffickers are very angry about some lost money, money that found its way to you. I think you must be very careful on your journey, very, very careful, Señor."

Tio shook Cody's hand, gave Victor a hug, and with tearful goodbyes all over the place, took off with Ramon in the direction from which they had all come.

The three of them, Cody, Victor and Mirabella, set out on that dewy, sunny morning to find their way to Cali and from there back to Miami. Maribella, who quickly announced her undying love for Cody, and soon after became his paramour, really knew her way in these rocky, mountainous parts. The landscape had changed. Now and then they saw a house, a *finca,* a little farmhouse, but for the most part there was nothing but rocky, untillable terrain.

It's amazing the tremendous crops of poppies grown for their obvious value. Where the hell do they grow? If it was on the hillsides that Victor and Cody encountered, they must survive on nothing. No fertilizer, no rain. Nothing. But, survive they must since it is the big agro-industry in Colombia. The biggest.

Of course, first chance he got, he asked Cody what the hell the old man was talking about, what kind of big bucks had come his way. He told Victor a rather large down payment was made in Miami before they left. And it was in a very safe place.

No one would ever believe it, but they walked and walked, sore feet, sore back, sore legs. It seemed they would never stop their arduous task. Day after day, they would go through one little village after another and there was always someone to give them a clean bed and some delicious food. They took their first bath outside the house, in a backyard, no real bathrooms in the campesino's houses. What a joy, even though it was with hard, dark brown soap, no lather, and it scratched like hell and smelled like lye. But their skin rejoiced and their psyche was renewed.

Over the next few weeks Cody spent more of their treasured stash of American money. It's amazing how poor some of these people are and the $100 bills were gleefully shared among many of the villages. They even sent people to accompany them to safety to the next small town or village. Really, they had escort service high up in the mountainous ridges of the Colombian Andes. It was so strange to actually see for themselves so much poverty, since it is a well known fact that 90 percent of all the emeralds in the world come from Colombia. Who the hell gets the money?

Cody never learned a word of Spanish. It was like his mind had closed tightly to any linguistic skill, and he rarely spoke, even to Victor, only when he had to. This trip was taking its toll and even though Victor had to admit at the time, he was terribly jealous of the obvious affection between Cody and Maribella, he was glad for the comfort he derived from her. She was a gentle and lovely person and at times being in her presence, they felt a Madonna-like quality about her. It was very interesting, but probably not unusual that Victor, being a Latino, was much more at ease during the whole trip than was Cody.

At least that was true once they got out of their prison. Victor's culture shock was not nearly the same as Cody's, even though he was as far away from home as he. They were in a homeland of sorts, where Victor's native language was spoken. But it was surprising because Cody was a soldier of fortune type of guy, fearless and usually comfortable no matter what the surroundings. And his little lady was apparently madly in love and taking care of all of his earthly erotic and intimate needs.

Victor had a lot of time to talk to their various guides. They plied him with questions, about America and Miami in particular, as they traveled across the rocky, hilly countryside. At times the terrain was rough with wide flat plateaus and gentle slopes. He asked questions also, curious as to where they were at the time. And the responses always varied, but for the most part he was told they were going north in the Andes, coming close to Cali, the big city near the Pacific coast, and from there they would move northeast up toward Medellin.

Several of the guides painted horrible pictures for Victor as to what would have happened had they gone before the *justicia.* They never would have gotten any kind of justice. The local authorities in many cases are the real power behind the drug trade.

They and the paramilitaries who are usually lawyers, judges and other rich people protect the cartels and the people who pay them off. And even worse things would happen if they were caught.

So the escape was a Godsend, and the only solution to survival. Unless, of course, some of the guerrillas caught up with them. That would mean the end. But they were moving to safety as fast as they could and luckily with lots of help.

The whole fuckin' place was filled with organized killers belonging to one group or another.

Colombia is a very large country divided into several regions. Some are jungle - the world's largest rain forest is in the Amazon Basin - and lots more jungle by the Orinoco River. Thank God they were not there. Then there is the Andes region, hilly, really mountainous, and of course, the two oceans, Atlantic and Pacific, grace the shoreline of Colombia, as well as the Caribbean Sea on the northern tip.

They were traveling north toward Cali in the mountainous region near the Andes. Cody told Victor the path of their trip would constantly be northward and a little to the east, after they left Cali toward Medellin. They were always on the alert for patrols of guerrillas or others who would like to capture them again.

Victor said that he had never seen a more joyous, friendly bunch of Latinos anywhere in the world. Their spirit of camaraderie was overwhelming.

A happier people would be hard to find in spite of the lack of the necessities that we in America take for granted. Most are Catholics who take their religion very seriously and enjoy the fiesta days that are related to the various saints who watch over and, they believe, provide for them.

Many of the people Victor and Cody encountered were definitely of mixed blood, Caucasian and Indian, which provided them with an external beauty that came through in their beautiful clear, coppery skin, their dazzling white teeth and shiny, ebony black hair.

So perhaps, Victor reckoned, all the things we have that we think really enhance our lives, aren't all that necessary.

Besides their obvious physical attractiveness, Victor was taken with their sense of hospitality, a sharing of all they had with them, who were really complete strangers to them in every way. Apart from his obvious Spanish heritage, he was totally alien to them and yet they treated him like a brother. Even Cody, remote and distant as he appeared was welcomed and treated well. He wondered about this for weeks and thought that perhaps it was because they came with money, that was surely no secret, but in his heart, he felt it was much more than that.

Finally, in one small community, really not even a village, but with a group of Colombian-Indios who lived together in one small settlement, he got part of the answer he was seeking. With all our modern telephones, we don't have a communication system that surpasses or even equals that of the *campesinos* all over Colombia. Each place they traveled to knew they were coming, each had a welcoming committee and they all knew their story. It was as if they had a secret society that transmitted the news on drums from village to village.

Hearing their version of their story sounded strange and exotic to Victor's ears. It went like this: An American airplane pilot, considered to be a hero, and his Spanish friend were crossing Colombia on foot. Their trip was a pilgrimage to take a beautiful but horribly disfigured señorita to a big city where she could be treated by doctors who would be paid by this man who loved her. This hero, an American, was willing to sacrifice his love for her in order to bring about her well-being and return her to the beauty she was before.

Seemed like they were becoming national folk heroes. But it served them well, and here's the real kicker. Since they were undoubtedly hiding from the *policia*, the drug traffickers and the guerrillas, as they would take their money and possibly even kill them, it was a real *problema*. They feared that if the worst happened, the girl would be lost to a lifetime of scarred ugliness, and therefore, at any cost, they had to be protected. So, a sort of underground jungle army took them under their collective wings and helped them to flee to the safety they sought.

In that rural, unsophisticated countryside where these folks had barely enough to feed themselves, the three of them were treated like visiting royalty. It was the feeling that ran through all of them that so impressed Victor, and Cody too. They were surprised that they were accepted so unequivocally. These were an open, guileless people, honest to themselves and to them, and it was refreshing.

When he hears stories now about the Colombian drug trade, and hears aspersions cast upon the people, he cringes to think how unfair it is that the taint of the drug cartel is tarring a whole country full of wonderful and innocent people with the same brush. Doubtless there are those among them who deal in the coca industry and certainly now more than ever, but, for the most part, they are a proud and honorable people.

It was decided for them that in the interest of safety, they would not actually go into Cali, but rather skirt the city and continue on toward Medellin, another several weeks' journey, the way they were doing it. From there they planned to go to a town called Pereira. It was quite a bit out of their way, as they had to go many miles to the west, but because of what they had found out from their "peon pipeline," it was a necessary change of direction for the time being. They would find safety there where they would remain for a few days with some of Tio's relatives.

Rumors were mushrooming in the depths of the Colombian jungle villages that they had escaped and the powers that be in Colombia put a big reward out for their capture, dead or alive. Scared the shit out of Victor when he heard that. Apparently, the search for them was escalating and they would have to go quickly to the next stopping place and lie low for a while. Traveling in the mountains, the lowlands and the forests was beginning to take its toll on them. They hungered for a little of the luxury they all took so much for granted. But Victor was exhilarated and actually feeling pretty good for all the wear and tear on him, and an extra bonus was that he had even slimmed down a bit. Nothing like a good long walk in the woods and mountains to get you in shape.

The local color was amazing; the exotic birds and plants and flowers they saw along the way were magnificent. They were not in the jungle, no parrots or macaws, but they saw lots and lots of hummingbirds, many different varieties. Some were so tiny you could hardly see them and had names like Sun Angels and Velvet Purple Coronets, tiny and swift moving. Seeing the lovely birds sure brightened their days. As for Cody, well, he never paid much attention to the wildlife. Considering that he was up with *la señorita* most of the night exhibiting his sexual prowess, which, on many nights, resulted in her singing like one of those tropical birds, he wasn't doing too badly.

Those pleasurable nights would not last very long. Indeed, the worst, most dangerous part of their adventure was yet to come.

Chapter Twenty-Nine

$\mathcal{T}$ he next few weeks flew by in flurries of movement interspersed with rest. They left for the trip to Medellin, where they would finally part company with the lovely Maribella. Victor wondered how Cody was going to deal with that, but had so many other things on his mind that he really gave it very little thought. After they finally arrived, they spent a week in Medellin, making all the arrangements for Maribella's surgery. Cody dropped a good deal of cash there with her relatives, and after lots of tearful goodbyes they prepared to leave Medellin.

That's when my story came into play. It was in Colombia that I spent the first night in a wonderful hotel in the heart of Medellin, in the area called *El Poblado*, the Poblado Plaza Hotel. It was not far from the extraordinary tourist attractions and the internationally known Plaza Botero.

From the moment I got out of the taxi at the hotel, I was sure I had been followed and was on a definite path to doom. I was just being crazy. No one knew or even gave a shit who I was or why I was there. But that had nothing whatsoever to do with my paranoia. Although it is commonly agreed that if it's true, you're not paranoid.

Who the hell knew what was true and what was not? Were a bunch of Colombian thugs so pissed off at Cody that they would find me and kill me or worse to find out what I knew? Well, let them. I really didn't know fuck at all, and I was only there to try to be a good friend and help those poor bastards out of an impossible situation. So I extricated myself from the back of that dilapidated taxi and dragged my shabby tan leather bag into the lobby of this magnificent old South American hotel. It was a sad sight, that bag, but it had gone many, many places with me and I could not bring myself to give it up.

My room was lovely with brightly colored paintings of tropical birds and an ornamental wrought iron balcony, which afforded me a splendid view of the northwest Andes Mountains. The first thing I did was draw a hot, luxurious bath. I could feel the tension seep out of me as soon as I slipped into the steamy water and found myself floating into a kind of semi-coma, my nostrils filled with the luscious fruity scent of the bath oil and my eyelids heavy with the weight of the world. At least with the weight of what was my world at the moment.

After a little eternity passed as I comfortably lolled in the bathtub, letting my whole being relax, my mind wandered easily to what the next few days might bring. Taking a look at my pink and wrinkled skin brought me out of my lethargy and I realized that I had better get out and back into what had rapidly become my real world.

A cozy nap and I'll be back in good spirits, I told myself just before drifting off to the land of dreams.

The jangling telephone, trying to throw itself off the hook, woke me up in what seemed like a week and a half later. Actually, the little gold clock that was shaped like an old Inca sun told me it was about an hour later.

"Hello, er *hola*," I stammered. "Yes, this is she, I mean me, yes, Señora Lanfield. Who is this?" I asked.

Rising up on a pretty sore elbow, I guessed I'd been sleeping on my arm and it was all pins and needles.

Again I asked, "Who is this? Oh, oh, yes of course, forgive me, I fell asleep. I was so tired."

The strident male voice, heavily accented and seemingly cold as the ice that had melted in my Piña Colada on the nearby tabletop, continued.

"So, you are here," he said, with almost a sigh changing the tone of his voice to a more gentle sound.

"Yes, I landed about – "

"We know, we checked your flight. Listen," he said, in a hurried manner, "we would like to meet

247

with you tonight. We will come to your hotel. Stay there." Click.

I didn't know what to expect.

I waited in my room until the desk clerk or as they say, *concierje* , rang my room and told me I had a caller waiting in the lobby. I was dressed in a silky sky blue blouse and a tight fitting pair of designer jeans, with an impressive pair of high style leather boots that I had bought a couple of summers before in Texas while I was there writing a big, juicy bond on a murder case. They cost me a week's pay, but were worth it. After I bought them and moaned about the cost, Sammy felt sorry for me and paid for them. That was one of the perks of having a brother in the business of making lots of money.

In the lobby waiting for me were two of the most attractive men I had ever seen, and one very lovely woman. Her hair was the color of jet and shiny as a raven's wing. Having been blond all my life, I've always envied women with dark hair. Somehow the brunette look always emphasized the eyes, either smoldering dark brown or misty light blue, the contrast was incredible. But, for whatever reason I stayed blond. And I was glad too.

I was especially glad at that moment, when these two incredibly handsome men looked at me like I was friggin' Marilyn Monroe. And, as I stepped down the last steps of the winding staircase, I felt like Marilyn Monroe. Yo.

"Señora Lanfield?" the taller of the two men inquired.

"Yes, I am Laura Lanfield," I managed in my most throaty voice.

Let's have a little fun here, I mused to myself. God only knows what's behind the next door.

"I am Juan Carlos," he said, with a bit of a twinkle in those gorgeous mahogany brown eyes. He was the caller, the voice on the telephone.

"May I present Jorge and his wife, Carlotta?" Obviously surnames were not to be part of this little drama."

"Okay, that's all right with me," I continued musing to myself.

Anyway, it really did not matter who the hell they were as long as they took me to Cody. I was still tired but that was the bottom line in this whole scenario.

We left the hotel after all the smiles and introductions and Juan Carlos, obviously the leader of this little entourage, said to me, "Tomorrow we are going to take you to where you want to be, but for tonight we thought you might prefer to relax. We are going to have a nice dinner and some good wine so we are going to a small café that we favor. It is nearby and we are sure you will enjoy it."

His English was good, understandable, but with an extraordinary sensual intonation like, God help me, Fernando Lamas in some old movies, and I was melting like a piece of Swiss cheese on a Reuben sandwich. He knew it too.

We walked to the café a few blocks away, just two very attractive, well dressed couples talking and laughing together. Who would ever guess the sinister plot that had brought us together, or the impending danger that could be waiting for all of us?

They were right. It was a lovely place to have dinner. Right there in El Poblado, a lovely quaint steakhouse called El Corral.

I told Juan Carlos in my rather halting Spanish that I would love for him to order my meal. He had no problem with that and assured me he would have them bring to the table such Colombian delicacies as I had never known. I felt a bit of double entendre there, and looked over at Carlotta and Jorge, but they were so lost in each other that I knew they were paying very little mind to Juan Carlos, me, or the ordering of food.

His taste in food, as his taste in clothes, was flawless, and before long we were dining on an excellent appetizer of the finest *escabeche* I had ever experienced. This was followed by a delicately spiced *sopa de pollo* and *sobre barriga*, a savory flank steak, perfectly prepared to my liking, rare but not very bloody.

How the hell did he know how I liked my steak? I wondered, since he never asked. I could just feel in my bones that he was the kind of man who knew what would please a woman, food, and everything else.

It seemed to me that all the food served in the most impeccable style was kind of spicy and perhaps designed to start a bit of fire in the blood. Whoo.

Stop it, I scolded myself. But my little heart was beating very rapidly and I knew it was a delicate balance I must maintain. On the one hand, I had to be appealing and let this man realize that I was a classy, game female. Certainly that was obvious since I had gotten my sweet ass over to Colombia for the sole purpose of getting my partner back safe and sound to the States.

On the other hand I thought, I must not let him think I was too game, too much of a player, or I'd end up in the sackeroo and Cody would really be the one to get fucked. Also, time was of the essence. Cody did not know I was in Colombia, in Medellin. And the question was how long he would be staying here in the city. Word had it that the girl had already left them. I was in a real quandary.

Ah, yes, dessert was a creamy delicate guava and mango flan with a carmellized sauce drizzled over it. And since Juan Carlos refilled my wine glass more times than I care to remember, I was eating this superb confection in a not exactly intoxicated state, but not far from it.

Was it the wine, the meal or him? I wondered very quietly.

In response to Juan Carlos asking me in a very intimate tone if I cared for an after-dinner drink, I replied, "Not if you don't want to carry me out of here."

He merely smiled that incredible smile of his and I felt that the seduction was complete.

That comment seemed to bring me out of my semi-hypnotized state. The enormity of the thought of having to be carried out of that restaurant was very sobering and indeed embarrassing.

251

Get a hold, girl, I reckoned, again quietly. And then with a smile, regained my composure. The room stopped spinning, the snowy white tablecloth was no longer a misty cloud and I was back in the here and now.

Silently, thank God. The trance was broken. Even Jorge and Carlotta felt it. The seduction would have to wait for another day.

With a cool, dignified but charming smile, I put the railroad back on its tracks and said to Juan Carlos, "If we are going to have an early start, this *señorita* must have some sleep. It's a far piece down the road from Miami to here."

God, he was sophisticated and incredibly pragmatic. In an instant his entire demeanor changed to courteous concern for my exhaustion and in a few minutes he smiled and said to the waiter, '*la cuenta, por favor*', and we were up and back out into the cool Medellin night air.

Actually, it was Jorge who, after our walk back to the Poblada Plaza hotel, said to me in more perfect English than I thought he knew, "It will be early when we arrive to take you to a meeting place, probably around five tomorrow morning. Please have your bags packed and come down to the lobby. I will arrange before we leave to have the *concierje* waken you by four o'clock."

He smiled and I felt dismissed, and was very relieved. I thanked all three of my hosts, and with a special smile for Juan Carlos, turned and dramatically swept myself up the marvelous staircase. Not only did I feel like Marilyn Monroe, but a bit of Scarlett O'Hara crept into my swagger as I turned back from halfway up the stairs to flash a last brilliant smile. God, I was drunk.

Dumb American broad, they were probably thinking. Who cared?

Well, this dumb broad was about to encounter some really heavy shit.

Chapter Thirty

I slept a wonderful dreamless sleep and awoke to the jingle of the telephone. I was refreshed, aware and excited. That wine must have been incredibly expensive. No headache. Cheap wines can sometimes affect me. But not this morning.

Downstairs I was disappointed to see only Jorge waiting for me in the lobby. I immediately felt that my hopes of seeing Juan Carlos would be dashed on the rocks of my infantile and transparent sensuality of the previous night. I was wrong.

Juan Carlos was in the car, and he welcomed me with that brilliant smile and the old Reuben sandwichy feeling returned in all its glory.

"We are going to take you to a church," he said. "That is where your friend will be this morning at six o'clock and you will join him and his other friend. I do not think he knows you are here, so please, try and be very calm, as we do not want to attract any more attention than is necessary."

He went on to tell me that neither Cody nor Victor looked quite the same as they did when they were arrested and I must make no loud outcries when I saw them. I assured him that I would retain my composure and we started on our short journey. The Church was no more than five minutes drive from the hotel and the very early Sunday morning Mass was about to begin when we arrived.

Jorge explained to me that they had a very early Mass one Sunday a month for people who traveled very far from the countryside the night before. In that way they could get an early start to return to their villages before nightfall. Made sense to me.

I covered my head with the black lacy, mantilla like shawl that I had brought for this purpose, having been told by certain family members that the meeting would probably be at a church.

At that moment I saw them. And it was a rude awakening. I would not have recognized them at first glance had I not been looking out for them. Cody was so blond and he had a full beard. Victor, who always felt he needed to be on a diet, had slimmed down and was very dark and handsome.

Then they saw me. At the same time. I had not changed.

The emotions that washed over me were incredible and I began to weep silently. They did not know I was coming. The family felt it might be dangerous to tell them, might have affected their judgment and possibly endangered them.

So it was a surprise.

Juan Carlos was on one side of me, Jorge on the other. I lifted my sunglasses and looked at my two dear American friends and it was an indescribable moment.

The plan was that Jorge would ask the two men to step outside of the church while I, who only went inside for the few moments it took for them to recognize me, went out to the car with Juan Carlos and waited. Apparently, Cody and Victor had been told by their hosts to go to the church at that time, but they did not know why.

Even though I was in Medellin, I had decided to stay away from my relatives, Jose and his wife, in the interest of their safety. They had done their work in letting us know about Victor and Cody and it would have been senseless to get them involved any further.

I went as quickly as I could to the car with Juan Carlos. But it was difficult going back through the courtyard because loads of people were pouring into the church and we felt like salmon trying to swim upstream. But the crowd was good. That was the whole idea. So far, so good.

In less than five minutes, Jorge appeared and Cody and Victor got into the backseat of Juan Carlos' Mercedes-Benz with me and Jorge in the front, and we were off like a lightning bolt.

No words were spoken by any of us. Then Victor asked, "Lori, what the hell are you doing here?" And we all laughed.

The tension was broken.

I said, "What the hell are *you* doing here?"

Jorge said, "Most importantly, we are going to get all three of you the hell out of here."

That surprised me because Jorge did not seem like the kind of guy who would use even a gentle expletive. One never knows, does one?

We drove for about 10 minutes to another part of the city, picked up two small backpacks that belonged to Cody and Victor, and then Juan Carlos drove us out of the city and we were to begin our journey home.

We said our goodbyes to the ever-gorgeous and sophisticated Juan Carlos and his good friend Jorge, and since by now it was late afternoon and nobody had eaten all day, we enjoyed a late lunch with our new compatriots. I did not know where we were exactly, only that it was on the way north toward our ultimate goal, Venezuela. Actually, we were just outside the city of Bello, in a farmhouse where we would remain for a few days with Luz and her husband Diego.

We ate marvelous Colombian food over the next few days. Cody and Victor were relaxed and comfortable and it was wonderful to be with them, and to have all of us safe. Plans were being made for our upcoming travel and I was amazed at the networking that was done.

Then the weather began to change, and it got a lot cooler; apparently it was fast becoming winter. You could tell by the rains every day. Winter is the wet season in that part of the world, and it comes and it goes, and summer is the dry season and it too comes and goes. There can be two months of wet winter followed by three or four months of dry summer. Strange, but that's how it is.

Our friends Luz and Diego arranged for us to have transport with a local truck driver who was heading north. It was not like traveling in Juan Carlos' Mercedes, but what the hell, it was warm in the truck and very roomy.

Victor and I spent a lot of time talking and he continued on with details of what had occurred before I got there.

He started with, "The last I remembered, it was late June in Miami Beach, and I was preparing to board an airplane in the dead of night at Opa-Locka Airport in Miami. Cody said we'd be going for a little trip and we would be back home in a few days. We were going to have a day or so of partying in South America with some beautiful dark-eyed beauties. Cody would get to fly one of his favorite airplanes, the Stretch 727, make a few bucks, and get us home in time for the big Fourth of July celebration. Yeah, only we got barbecued and the fireworks were all pointed at us. We celebrated our country's birthday, and mine as well, in a tiny cage on a hot day in the ass end of Colombia."

I stopped him with, "Oh well, with any luck we'll soon be out of here and you'll have only memories of your reckless adventure and life-saving trek through a goodly part of South America."

So, he shut up for the time being.

We arrived safely, and had a week in the lovely area of Bucaramanga, where we stayed with a cousin of Mirabella's uncle Tio. Tio had earned our trust, so we had no trepidation. I was amazed at how far flung their family was and how many of them there were. I came to find out later that cousin is a word that is very much misinterpreted, having really nothing, *nada*, to do with bloodlines. Kissing cousins in America is the closest we come to what they mean. Victor told me about Maribella and the travel adventures they shared and I was really surprised to discover that Cody was incredibly shaken by the loss of that little lady. He really did care for her in a very special way.

We continued on north now - I had been in Colombia about six weeks at that point - and our next stop would be Cucuta just before the Venezuelan border, and from there on to our final destination, San Cristobal, a mountainous region of Venezuela just across the border from Colombia. Our friends had decided long ago that it would be too difficult to get us on an airplane to fly home from Colombia. It would be much safer from Venezuela. We certainly did not have any objections. Looking back I have to admit that it was an unbelievable adventure and it was especially so for Cody and Victor who had spent all those months traveling in serious danger. It was still dangerous for yours truly, but no one was looking for me and I became the perfect shill.

Victor told me that the last part of the trip, while I was with them, was actually the most exciting for him. First of all, he had all of Cody's attention. He was missing Maribella, and was more open and friendly to Victor than he had been in months. And the trip to San Cristobal in the province of Tachira was really marvelous.

New at this game, but catching on fast, I was getting used to walking, and we knew how to get our rest. Our guides were a bit more sophisticated and Cody and Victor's folk hero reputation preceded us and made the going easy.

I often wondered what the *campesinos* thought of la *rubia*, Spanish for blond woman, who was now part of the scene. In a rare moment of disclosure, Cody told me he was so happy that he had given the family where Maribella was going to stay a thousand of our most precious dollars. Because of that, arrangements were being made for the plastic surgery on her face. The deed was done. He was also tickled that I had brought money and fattened our pot. Good luck travels with those who have some loot. We never forgot that the possibility was always there that for a few American dollars we could have been betrayed and even killed.

Christmas had been a strange one for us, spent with Colombian *campesinos* and Indios, Christians all, but lots of things we were used to were lacking. Their idea of Christmas was not like ours, but charming, and certainly because of the religious aspects the true spirit of Christ came through. Gifts were meager but heartfelt, and the music was very much the Latin beat of a cha-cha, meringue or salsa. Perhaps a mix of all of them, but delightful. The hymns were sung and the children blessed and all in all it was a most unique event for Cody, Victor and me. I never forgot for a moment what deadly danger we were in.

In an astonishing moment of reflection, Victor said, "We have been away from home a very long time. We have skillfully and with the help of our mentors avoided being captured again and for that we were grateful. We are slimmer, tanner and who knows, perhaps a little wiser for all of our travels."

And then he added, "One thing is sure, nothing for me but commercial airlines from now on."

Surprisingly, Cody said he felt the same. But I wouldn't put any money on that one.

The trip to San Cristobal was exciting. The family that accompanied us were professionals. The father and mother, *Señor* and *Señora* Delgado, were *doctores* and their 20-something son was a student at the university and going for his degree in engineering. Their teenage daughter, Solara, a budding little dark eyed beauty with all the attributes of a fiery, steamy, but yet untried sexpot, attempted many, many times to catch Victor's eye. Perhaps something sexual would have happened had he had different feelings. Although a gentleman to the umpteenth degree, Victor would have never allowed any sensuality on his part or on the part of the lovely young *señorita* to compromise his position with all of us, but it was out of the question anyway. I had come to realize that his proximity to Cody only enhanced his love and admiration for him, and it was quite obvious to me that Cody was all he really wanted. I think the mother caught on to that, but in a typical cultured Latin way, understood and said nothing of it.

She tried to convince her daughter that Victor was far too old for her and would soon be leaving for America and his own life. In a way she made Victor even more attractive to the lusty little *señorita*.

Traveling with these *gentes importantes*, important people, made our going a bit easier and a hell of a lot more upscale, and about time after nearly two months of hard, perilous travel. We took a bus across the border into San Cristobal. Our stories were ready for any border patrols, but there were none, and to tell the truth Cody and Victor hardly looked like the two *gringos* of many months ago, and of course I was still the perfect foil. Cody had a long beard, which he wore with pride, and his natural inclination to be quiet served him well. No one really spoke to him. When there was talking to be done, it was done by the family or by Victor.

I must say Cody looked very attractive with his beard and long hair. The sun had bleached it until it was very light and his electric blue eyes shone with an intensity that made people stare at this handsome, quiet, almost enigmatic person.

San Cristobal was a bustling city located in the Venezuelan province of Tachira. We arrived there in mid-January, apparently just in time for their *Rio Carnaval*-type fiesta called *Feria,* and the streets were decorated with brightly colored lights and music played all day and into the night. It was good for us to be there at that time because if anyone was looking for us in those crowds, we'd be impossible to spot, even with Cody's blue eyes. I saw many blond and blue-eyed South Americans from other parts of the country at the fiesta, and so we got by with our little ploy of integrating with the party-goers.

Our plan called for us to stay two nights at the home of *Senor* and *Senora* DeLaCruz, a wealthy rancher and his family who were friends of *Senor* and *Senora* Delgado, our hosts and patrons for this last leg of the journey. We saw a real *rancho grande*, there on the outskirts of San Cristobal where our host family lived, and for the first time in many months, I could see that Cody and Victor relaxed their guard and actually felt comfortable with our friends and our friends' friends.

That night in a big comfortable bed by myself, I dreamed the dreams of the innocent and prepared for the next day and our flight to Miami. The good night's sleep did wonders for all of us, and refreshed and renewed, we came down to a wonderful Spanish *desayuno*. Breakfast was mostly fruit, exotic fruits I had come to know and to love, mangoes, papaya, guanabana, with its sweet, milky taste, and of course bananas, such as I had never seen, tiny and red and utterly delicious. Sausage, prepared to perfection, and eggs pampered with a wonderful, spicy salsa.

Also, there was a warm, fragrant bread, topped with some fruit jelly that I had never tasted and its sweet yet pungent taste made my lips pucker. The family laughed at me and said legend has it that if you eat that fruit jelly and it puckers your lips, you will be the next to marry. And, of course, coffee. The whole time we were in Colombia we drank lots of coffee, *café*. And it was delicious, strongly brewed with a hint of sugar. But this was something entirely different. More like a *café con leche*, sweetened and rich with cream and a hint of cinnamon. Marvelous.

Our host and hostess were very interested in what had transpired on our trip through Colombia, and asked a lot of questions. They had relatives living there and were very concerned about the deteriorating conditions because of the drug cartels. It was astonishing that they, knowing our story - and it seemed that everyone in that part of the world did by now - were able to host us in such a hospitable manner. The bottom line of the whole goddamn thing was that Cody had gone to Colombia to bring back drugs. Somehow, their act of valor had, in the eyes of these people, whitewashed them clean as the driven snow. Long live mercy.

Soon it was arranged that we would meet up with some of Dr. Delgado's Venezuelan compatriots at the Iglesia De Los Recolletos, a very famous and popular church in San Cristobal. The trusted *amigo de nuestro corazon* was a taxi driver who would whisk us away from the crowds and to the safety of the airport. Once again, it was decided that for the time being, keeping us in the midst of tourists with lots of activity going on around us would ensure our security. So, on this, our last day in South America, Victor, Cody, and I traveled once again in a beautiful Mercedes-Benz to where we would meet these trusted people.

Only Mr. And Mrs. De La Cruz accompanied us, so we made our tearful farewells to these new friends, the Delgados, who had looked after us so well.

Driving around the cathedral three or four times, each time approaching it from another direction, Señor De La Cruz finally came to a quick stop and in moments we were hustled into a beat up old taxi for the ride to the airport. What can I say about the ride to the airport? For the most part it was uneventful, except for the driver who drove like three kinds of maniac. Not your casual slip-out-of-town venture at all.

Cody, Victor, and I, in that short 30 minutes, re-lived in our minds much of what had happened to us in the past few months. It was a helter-skelter trip down a memory lane that was to live in my thoughts forever.

We had been given airline tickets in our own names. Copies of Cody's and Victor's passports had been obtained from the American Embassy in Venezuela and were delivered to us by the De La Cruzes. My passport was just fine. Everything was in order. As we bid farewell, this time to our most reverent and solicitous taxi driver, and walked out to the tarmac to board the waiting 737. The terror was still very much with us. I tried to be calm, but my heart was pounding with fear and apprehension.

For Chrissakes, what if the policia were hiding and waiting for us? What if the taxi driver was paid to turn us over to the drug dealers?

My mind was overcome with worry as we walked down the tarmac to that fuckin' airplane. *Look at all the agony and torment we've lived through. Why we've both been in jeopardy since we landed here.* I thought to myself.

I was delighted to leave it all behind.

"What about you Cody?" I asked.

He looked at me for a long while and wistfully said, "I guess I am."

Chapter Thirty-One

How could anyone in good conscience knowingly accept that her partner was a drug dealer? Cody made it very easy for me by being the person he was, cool, sophisticated in a boyish way, and always so charming. I realized it was impossible for me to defend his innocence any longer.

Now was the time for me to make a decision. I thought of all possible ways that I could approach the situation. On the very next day, I decided I would keep my eyes open for some event or occurrence that was bound to transpire between us, and then I would bring up all that was on my mind. I thought time was on my side. I did not know how little time was left.

I tried very hard over the next few days to pretend everything was the same. But it was very hard on me. Every time I looked at Cody, parts of the story flashed before me like fireworks on the

Fourth of July. The landing near the jungle, the bizarre circumstances of his arrest, the beautiful scarred girl. I wondered if she had undergone the operation and was restored to the incredible beauty Victor said she would be.

I wondered if Cody ever thought of her, and I wondered at his impassive, imperturbable, seemingly apathetic emotionless attitude. Maybe that was why I felt there was such a difference in Cody when I met him on my arrival in Colombia.

Perhaps a light had gone out deep inside of him. It was all beginning to make sense to me and I longed to speak out, reach out, and tell him that I understood.

At times I withdrew into myself and quietly stared at him, wondering how he could appear so self possessed with all the secrets he carried around. He never seemed to notice, or if he did, made no mention of it.

By nature, I am a passionate woman, very intense, but at the same time, outgoing and extroverted, as many Scorpios can be. For me it was a kind of signature. That was what started to give me away. This quietude I had adopted was foreign to me but noticed by my associates.

One afternoon I was alone in the office with Victor and I told him that I was thinking of making a break from Cody. I said that for too long I had suspected him of being very involved with drugs and it was beginning to upset me to where I could not continue with the lie.

He just looked at me and hugged me gently, and it was as if we both had a portent of what was to come, an omen, unspoken but silently displacing our equilibrium.

One Monday morning about two weeks later, Cody came to the office in a bright and chipper mood, as if suddenly all had gone well with the whole, wide world.

"Lori," he said, "Wednesday you and Jack can fly up to the land with me, it's ready for sale, and you can have your pick of the acreage." He pondered a moment and then said, "There's a wooded twenty up by the northeast corner, prime land, three acres already cleared for building on and . . ."

I burst in, "Cody, that's great, I'll call Jack."

He smiled and walked out of the office, calling over his shoulder, "Be ready at 10 o'clock at Opa-Locka Airport. We'll take the Mooney, it's at MAC."

Those were the last words he ever spoke to me, and the last time I ever saw him.

Tuesday morning, Jack and I went to the bank to arrange some financing for the land, and late that night Cody's daughter, Nancy, called me at home to say that her dad was dead. His new helicopter exploded in mid-air and he crashed and burned to death near the Everglades on his way home from the land. He was alone. Cody had died as he had lived, alone.

Overcome with grief and shock, I moved through the next morning in a trance-like state and couldn't leave the house. Victor called me about noon that Wednesday, the day we were to fly with Cody, and told me what he knew of the accident.

"Please spare me the grim details," I begged him, and through his tears he asked me to meet him for lunch at our favorite deli on the Beach.

"Give me an hour, and I'll be there."

He agreed and hung up, leaving me alone once again with this incredible sadness. It's a phenomenon that comes to all of us at one time or another, and though we react differently, it's always the same. The sudden, unexpected death of a friend or relative comes with a shock unique to that situation. There are no words, no feelings, except possibly an unrelenting pain that goes along with the tremulous, incredible emptiness that washes over you. We try for a why or wherefore, but it is never there, only the exquisite anguish that reaches into our soul and then beyond.

Cody was only 45. He had just had a birthday.

Some time later, from behind dark sunglasses, Victor and I looked at each other and smiled the pretend smile we are conditioned to do upon greeting a friend, regardless of the circumstances. Once we got past that we stared into each other's sorrowful, reddened eyes, and I said, "What happened to him, what really happened? We both know there is more to this than what we've, what you've been told."

And as we both wept sad and bitter tears, Victor said, "You're right, and tragically, apart from those who may have been involved, no one will ever know the truth." He pondered for a moment and then said, "It was simply an extremely unfortunate accident, something that should not have happened, but did."

That was no consolation for either of us. Victor was beside himself with grief and I could do no more than listen to his sad tale of the events as he had heard them from Cody's wife.

Victor started to speak softly.

"Apparently, Cody had taken the helicopter up for a trial run to look at the land from another perspective and was to be back later in the afternoon on Tuesday. He had planned to take you and Jack up on Wednesday, and incidentally, had invited me along as well, since I was interested in perhaps getting a parcel of the land for myself. He called his wife about five in the afternoon and said he was heading back to Miami. He must have taken a long route back because the next thing she heard about Cody was at seven thirty that night, a call from the air patrol telling her that there had been an accident in the Everglades. The helicopter, apparently to avoid crashing into a home on the edge of the Everglades, had gone into some trees and exploded. It was not in mid-air, actually, although the first explosion seemed to occur while he was still flying. There will be an investigation, of course, but what the hell, he's dead. Old crash-and-burn Williams finally met the big demon in the sky."

There was a memorial service for Cody on Sunday, but, since he had been literally cremated in the crash, burned beyond recognition, the family decided on a more-or-less non-funeral and no one was invited to attend except for a few close friends and family. That ended the saga of Cody Williams, and the part he played in our lives.

His wife collected some insurance and sold the land very quickly. Jack and I, under the circumstances, did not want to buy any of it. In a few months, I, as his partner, and beneficiary of the business, was supposed to receive the money Cody had put up when we started the bonding agency.

I was shocked to discover that, somehow, he had manipulated a loan against the deposit and there was only $200 left in the built-up fund. I was a bit bemused about that, but I'd had it with the bail bonds business.

Victor seemed devastated by Cody's death and eventually moved to San Francisco, where he passed the bar in California and practiced criminal law. I tried to locate him after about a year, but, despite my expertise in tracking people down, I was unable to find a listing for him anywhere.

Years later I heard from an attorney friend in Montana that Cody Williams did not die in that helicopter crash. He said he had heard that it was all staged so that he could escape both his drug dealing associates and the DEA, who were catching up fast. It seems that his hidden airport on the land, as well as his long runway, were not the secrets he imagined they were.

The attorney went on to tell me that rumor had it that Cody was living somewhere in Mexico with his homosexual lover.

It sounded like Elvis revisited and I didn't want to hear any more about it. Personally, I felt it was just like what Cody and Victor would do. It sure as hell would explain what happened to all the mysterious money that Cody had gotten prior to his Colombian adventure.

I was personally shattered by Cody's death. Whatever and whoever he was being made out to be didn't interest me. I knew the better, gentler side of him and I knew I would miss him a lot.

I never wrote another bail bond for the rest of my life.

THE END

www.ingramcontent.com/pod-product-compliance
Lightning Source LLC
Chambersburg PA
CBHW060839280326
41934CB00007B/841